VOCABULARY DEVELOPMENT

by

Steven A. Stahl

The University of Georgia

Volume 2 in the series
From Reading Research to Practice

Brookline Books

Other titles in this series:

1. When Adolescents Can't Read
2. Vocabulary Development
3. Language and Reading Success
4. Learning to Read in the Computer Age.
5. Reading and Linguistic Development

ISBN 1-57129-072-9

Library of Congress Cataloging-In-Publication Data
Stahl, Steven A.
        Vocabulary development / by Steven A. Stahl.
            p.   cm. – (From reading research to practice : v. 2)
        Includes bibliographical references and index.
        ISBN 1-57129-072-9 (pbk.)
            1. Vocabulary–Study and Teaching (Elementary)–United States.
    2. Vocabulary–Study and Teaching (Secondary)–United States.
    3. Reading comprehension.   I. Title.   II. Series.
    LB1574.S68 1998
    372.62–dc21   98-19330
                                                            CIP

Book design and typography by Erica L. Schultz.

Printed in USA by P.A. Hutchison Co.
10 9 8 7 6 5 4
Brookline Books
P.O. Box, 1209
Brookline, MA. 02445

Order Toll Free
Pathway Book Service
800-345-6665

Contents

Preface

This book — part of a new series, *From Reading Research to Practice* — is designed to bring to those working in the field of reading and literacy the most significant research underlying effective practices in reading instruction. Written for teachers of reading, this series will also be a valuable resource for prospective teachers, administrators, and researchers who seek to understand the new as well as the enduring research in the teaching of reading.

Nearly 100 years ago, Edward L. Thorndike, the most eminent educational psychologist of his time, did a deceptively simple study of the errors children made in answering questions designed to test their understanding of reading selections. He found that those students who had difficulty understanding a selection did not know the meanings of the words used in the selections.

His study had a profound effect on the teaching of reading. It contributed to the growing emphasis on teaching word meanings, particularly in the intermediate grades and higher. It also contributed to the research and application of readability from the 1920s to today, and established vocabulary difficulty as the best predictor of text readability.

In this book, Steven Stahl brings together the classic and new views on vocabulary and reading comprehension. He evaluates those views from the standpoint of research and practice, and suggests those practices that have the most beneficial effects in the classrooms and clinics of today.

Jeanne S. Chall, Ph.D., *Series Editor*
John F. Onofrey, *Editor*

Introduction

Four Questions

This little book is about words — words that you probably know, like *protein,* *catalytic,* or *protest;* words that you may know, like *actuary, palaver, palindrome,* or *Rastafarian;* or obscure words or jargon such as *minatory, adjuvant, hermeneutics,* or *paranomasia.* Our knowledge of words like these determines how we understand texts, define ourselves for others, and define the way we see the world. A richer vocabulary does not just mean that we know more words, but that we have more complex and exact ways of talking about the world, and of understanding the ways that more complex thinkers see the world. A simple example comes from Berlin and Kay's (1969) study of color terms. They found that the more advanced the civilization, the more differentiations its members made between different colors. Using the same box of colored chips, some societies classified each chip as either dark or light, some as dark, light or red, some adding green, etc. to the fine distinctions that we might make between a teal green and a kelly green. The more words we know, the more distinctions we make about the world, the more clearly we see things in our world. Understanding, for example, the distinctions between *protest* and *rebellion* is to understand the causes of the American Revolution and Tiananmen Square, how one side's protest became the other's rebellion, thus leading to accelerating conflict. We use words to think; the more words we know, the finer our understanding is about the world.

Since the time of Edward L Thorndike (1917), when scientific methodology had begun to be applied to the study of human thought, psychologists and educators have studied people's knowledge of word meanings and how they relate to other aspects of human thought. Perhaps much of this interest derives from the central role of vocabulary knowledge in so many aspects of mental behavior. Vocabulary knowledge is related to reading comprehension, intelligence, content area knowledge, and reasoning. Much of the research conducted since Thorndike's time has centered around four questions:

- What is the relationship between vocabulary knowledge and reading comprehension?

- How many words do people know?
- What does it mean to "know" a word?
- How do people learn words from context?

Our answers to these questions will help us to understand what kind of vocabulary instruction we should have if we want to improve students' comprehension.

If, for example, knowledge of word meanings directly affects comprehension, then the number of difficult word meanings in a text will be a good measure of the text's difficulty. This is the theory behind many readability formulas, nearly all of which use a vocabulary difficulty measure, often in conjunction with a sentence length measure (Zakaluk & Samuels, 1988). Similarly, if vocabulary knowledge directly affects comprehension, then teaching word meanings should improve students' ability to read more complex texts. This is the theory underlying most vocabulary teaching programs. But if vocabulary knowledge is not directly related to comprehension, but instead is related to a third factor, such as prior knowledge or ability, then we might direct our instructional time to other aspects of reading.

Similarly, if the number of words a person learns during a year in school is manageable, say 500 to 1000, then we can teach directly all the words that a person needs to know. If the number of words that a person learns in a year far exceeds that number, say 3000 or more, then we need to make other provisions for word learning.

Understanding these questions allows us to make intelligent choices about what words we teach, how we teach them, and how much time to devote to vocabulary instruction. The purpose of this book is, first, to discuss questions about vocabulary knowledge that underlie practice, and, second, to describe methods of teaching word meanings. My goal is to have teachers (and prospective teachers) understand the issues involved in teaching vocabulary, and through their understanding, be able to make informed choices about teaching. It is for that reason that I will begin by discussing these questions, followed by a discussion of how to teach word meanings.

Chapter 1

What Is The Relationship Between Vocabulary Knowledge And Reading Comprehension?

The importance of vocabulary knowledge for reading comprehension should be self-evident to anyone who has ever read a jargon-filled text, then scratched her head and wondered what she had just read. For example, here are three sentences from an early draft of a paper for a professional journal. (It has since been revised.)

> The findings of our study also reveal that there is nothing especially difficult about setting up a mental representation for a new lexical item as presumably children would have to do for unknown words. For example, for localist versions of connectionist viewpoints, it seems probable that one would first have to create a new lexical node before orthographic, phonological, and semantic information could become connected with it. Presumably, if substantiating a mental representation for a new lexical item was particularly difficult, we would expect to see that the development of unknown words was slower than for partial knowledge words because partial knowledge words already have an existing lexical node with corresponding orthographic and phonological features but few semantic features. [1]

To understand this paragraph, a reader must know the meanings of words such as *localist, connectionist, lexical, node, substantiating,* and so on. Without that knowledge, this paragraph would be gibberish. One of the oldest findings in educational research is the strong relationship between vocabulary knowledge and reading comprehension. All the evidence from correlational studies, readability research, and experimental studies reflects strong and reliable relationships be-

---

[1] This was taken from a draft version of an article. I am withholding the reference out of embarrassment.

tween the difficulty of words in a text and text comprehension (see Anderson & Freebody, 1981; Graves, 1986).

Does Vocabulary Knowledge Cause Comprehension?

If so, why is there such a relationship? The most obvious implication is that knowing word meanings enables or causes a person to comprehend a text containing those words. In this view, a person who knows the words can comprehend the text, regardless of any other factors. Anderson and Freebody referred to this as the "instrumentalist hypothesis," which is shown in Figure 1 below.

This hypothesis is fairly straightforward — knowledge of words *causes* readers to comprehend text. This has two implications. First, if word knowledge helps people to understand texts, then texts with more difficult words would be more difficult to understand. This is the basis of most readability formulas, which use a measure of word difficulty and a measure of sentence length to infer a text's relative difficulty. A person using the Dale-Chall Readability formula, for example, calculates the number of words not on a list of 3000 words presumed to be known by an average fourth-grader, then calculates the number of words per sentence, and using a formula or a chart, estimates the difficulty of the text. All readability formulas use some sort of vocabulary measure; some use only a vocabulary measure (Chall & Dale, 1995; Zakaluk & Samuels, 1988).

The second implication is that teaching word meanings should improve comprehension. Although not all methods of teaching word meanings do improve comprehension, overall vocabulary instruction does improve comprehension (Stahl & Fairbanks, 1986). Effective vocabulary instruction will be discussed in Chapter 5.

Vocabulary and Prior Knowledge

Knowing the meanings of the words in a passage may not be enough. It is possible to know all the words in a passage and still not make any sense of it.

Figure 1.
The instrumentalist hypothesis.

Vocabulary Knowledge ————————➤ **Reading Comprehension**

Consider the following passage taken from a Melbourne, Australia, newspaper:

> A hair raising century by Australian opener Graeme Wood on Friday set England back on its heels in the third test at the Melbourne Cricket Ground. Unfortunately, living desperately cost the Australians the match. Wood was caught out of his crease on the first over after lunch. Within ten more overs, the Australians were dismissed. Four were dismissed by dangerous running between creases. Two were dismissed when the English bowlers lifted the bails from the batsmen's wickets. The three remaining batsmen were caught by English fieldsmen. One was caught as he tried for a six. When the innings were complete, the Australians had fallen short of the runs scored by the English (cited in Hayes & Tierney, 1981, p. 265).

Even though we understand words like *crease, six, century,* and so on, this passage makes no sense unless we also know about the sport of cricket. Similarly, the words in the passage on page 3 are jargon from cognitive psychology and make no sense unless you understand the grander theories being discussed. Anderson and Freebody (1981) also advanced a *knowledge hypothesis,* according to which word meanings themselves do not cause people to understand texts. Rather, our knowledge of words reflects our knowledge of the topic. It is this knowledge of the topic that helps us comprehend. Thus, words like *century* have specific meanings when we are talking about cricket, and it is these meanings that help us understand the text. The knowledge hypothesis states that vocabulary knowledge is related to topic knowledge, which, in turn, is related to reading comprehension, as shown in Figure 2 below.

Obviously, people who know a great deal about a topic also know its vocabulary. Word meanings are not just unrelated bits of information, but are part of larger knowledge structures. A person who knows what a "jib" or a

Figure 2.
The knowledge hypothesis.

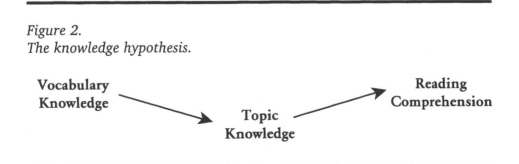

"spar" is might also know a lot about sailing, and thus might have a greater understanding of sailing than a person less versed in that area. Indeed, some researchers have used vocabulary tests to measure prior knowledge (e.g., Johnston, 1984).

Some people (e.g., Nagy, 1988) have suggested that it is important to teach words as part of semantic groups, so that students will understand how each word fits into a larger knowledge terrain. However, studies have not yet found that teaching words in semantic groups has any advantage over teaching words outside of such groups (e.g., Stahl, Buridge, Machuga, & Stecyk, 1992). Still, many successful vocabulary teaching techniques do teach words in semantic groups (Heimlich & Pittelman, 1992).

Vocabulary and General Ability

Vocabulary knowledge is also strongly related to intelligence. Terman (1916) said that if he could test only one factor to determine a person's IQ, he would choose vocabulary, because of its strong relation to overall intelligence. Because intelligence is also related to reading comprehension, it could be that vocabulary tests are actually measuring children's intelligence, which in turn is affecting their ability to read texts, as in the *general ability hypothesis* pictured in Figure 3 below. In this hypothesis, the correlations between vocabulary and comprehension are due to their relations to general ability, or that more able people have both greater vocabularies and are better able to comprehend texts.

In another variation of this hypothesis, Sternberg (1987) includes a factor in his model of intelligence of learning from context. That is, he suggests that there is a general ability to learn from context, both words and information. People who are higher in this ability are better able to learn words, since most words are learned from context, but they are also more able to perform other

Figure 3.
The general ability hypothesis.

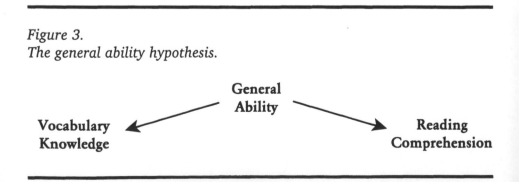

intelligent tasks. Sternberg and Powell (1983) attempted to teach adults general strategies for learning from context, with the aim of improving their vocabulary abilities and intelligence, but with mixed results.

Which of these hypotheses are true? In some way, all three say something about vocabulary and comprehension. Vocabulary knowledge certainly affects comprehension, because we do have evidence that teaching word meanings directly affects comprehension. Vocabulary knowledge is certainly related to topic knowledge, as should be evident from the article about cricket. Furthermore, vocabulary knowledge is related to intelligence, although the nature of that relationship is far from clear.

For a teacher, though, the instrumentalist hypothesis is the most important because it suggests that teaching word meanings will improve a child's comprehension. Stahl and Fairbanks (1986) found that vocabulary instruction does directly improve comprehension, thus validating the instrumentalist hypothesis. Furthermore, they found that not all approaches to teaching word meanings will improve comprehension. Before reviewing approaches to the teaching of word meanings, though, it would be useful to discuss three other questions that illuminate instructional issues.

Chapter 2

How Many Words Do People Know?

At first glance, this question might seem rather esoteric. After all, why should we care how many words people know when our concern is to teach the words they find in the texts they are reading? This question, however, is at the core of many other questions. If an average high school senior knows 45,000 words, according to one estimate (Nagy & Anderson, 1984), then it might not be possible to teach someone all the words he or she needs to know through direct instruction. If the estimate is closer to 17,000, as other authors have suggested (D'Anna, Zechmeister, & Hall, 1991), or even 5000 (Hirsh & Nation, 1992), then direct teaching might play a more important role. This is especially true for speakers of other languages who are learning English.

There are two ways of looking at the question of how many words people know: looking at texts that people read and testing people. Although estimates vary widely as to how many total words there are in English (unabridged dictionaries can have between 250,000 and 500,000 entries, depending on what they allow as entries), we have good data as to the number of words in books used by elementary and secondary students. Our best estimate, taken from Nagy and Anderson (1984), is that there are roughly 88,700 word families used in books up to 12th grade. A *word family* is defined by Nagy and Anderson as groups of words in which someone knowing one of the words (in the family) could guess or infer the meaning of the others when encountering it in context while reading, such as *add, addition, additive, adding,* and so on.

About half of the texts we read consist of the 107 most common words. Another 5,000 words account for the next 45%, so that 95% of the texts we read consist of about 5,100 different words (Adams, 1990). The rest of the texts we read consist of the remaining 83,000 or so words (Nagy & Anderson, 1984). If this is so, then why do we not just teach the 5,100 most common words and not worry about the relatively rare words? There are two problems with this logic. First, these "rare" words are not so rare. They are words that every literate adult should know and assumes that other literate adults do know. Words in this group might include *beneficial, advocate, accountant, cancer,* and so on. The second problem is that these "rare" words carry most of the content of the texts. How much would one understand in a biology text dealing with the discovery of penicillin without knowing such rare words as *penicillin, antibiotic, bacterium,* and so on? Many, but not all, of the uncommon words have to do with the particular topic of the text. This is especially true in the content areas. Words such as *abiotic, ecosystem,* and *niche* are relatively uncommon, but also very useful to have a useful understanding of ecology.

It is instructive to look at the number of words in texts that students read, but this does not tell us how many words an average student knows. We do know that this number is considerably less than 88,700, but it is not clear how much less. Early estimates varied wildly, from 17,000 to more than 200,000 words estimated as known by university undergraduates, or from 2,562 to 26,000 words estimated as known by first-graders (Lorge & Chall, 1963). Since one cannot ask a person every word he or she knows (can you imagine sitting down to a 90,000-item multiple choice test?), tests need to be based on samples. But the larger the dictionary that is used to sample from, the larger the estimate will be of a person's word knowledge; therefore, dictionaries of different sizes are partly responsible for these differences (see Lorge & Chall, 1963, for an explanation).

Even with a low estimate of 17,000 words, a researcher cannot ask students to define every word they supposedly should know. Even a test of 100 words is likely to be so fatiguing that the test would not be accurate. Thus every study that estimates the number of words known uses a sample. Usually this sample comes from a dictionary, possibly the fifth word from every 40th page.

The differing estimates of vocabulary knowledge are crucial to making decisions about vocabulary instruction. Because my experience and those of my colleagues suggest that 300-500 words per year can reasonably be taught through direct instruction (8–10 words per week, 50 weeks a year), the figure accepted is important in determining how to plan for vocabulary growth. If a teacher accepts Nagy and Anderson's (1984) estimate that there are 88,700 word types in English, and that students learn about half of them, this suggests that the average child learns about 3,000 new words each year. (There is other independent evidence that, indeed, children do learn about 3,000 new words per year; White, Graves, & Slater, 1990.) Even doubling or tripling our estimate for direct vocabulary teaching, we cannot reach 3,000 words per year through direct teaching alone. Most of these words learned must come from context (Sternberg, 1987). However, if you accept a lower figure, such as the 17,000 words suggested by D'Anna et al. (1991), or about 1000 new words per year, then it may be possible to teach all the words that a person needs to learn. This distinction is especially important in teaching English as a second language (Gouldman, Nation, & Read, 1990). ESL students rely more heavily on direct instruction than native speakers, because they typically need to make up more ground more quickly to learn English.

If we take a higher estimate for the number of words that children learn each year, will contextual reading be enough to learn 3,000 words per year? This is a monumental task, requiring the learning of about eight words a day, every day, and twice that many if word learning occurs only on school days. Nagy and his colleagues (Nagy, Herman, & Anderson, 1985; Nagy, Anderson, & Herman, 1987; Herman, Anderson, Pearson, & Nagy, 1987) have calculated that much of this annual growth in reading can come from incidental learning of word meanings. Their argument goes as follows:

- We assume that a fifth-grade child reads for an hour per day (in and out of school) at a rate of 150 words per minute (a conservative estimate; see Harris & Sipay, 1990), 5 days a week, then the child will have encountered 2,250,000 words in the course of all this reading.
- If 2% to 5% of those words are unknown (as in instructional level text; Betts, 1946), the child will have encountered from 45,000 to 112,500 unknown words.
- From other research, we know that children will learn between 5% and 10% of previously unknown words from a single reading (Nagy & Herman, 1987).
- This would account for at least 2,250 new words learned from context each year.

Making all the estimates as conservative as possible, the 2,250 new words is close enough to 3,000 to suggest that context can be a powerful influence on students' vocabulary growth. This suggests that one of the most powerful things we can do to increase children's vocabulary is to encourage them to read as widely as possible.

However, what if we accept the lower estimate of 1,000 words per year? Although our estimates show that children usually can be taught 300 to 400 words per year (8 to 10 words per week, 40 weeks a year), with more intensive vocabulary instruction this number could be doubled. Thus, we might be able to teach nearly all the words an average child learns in a year through direct instruction.

Differences in Word Knowledge

Either set of estimates to determine children's knowledge of word meaning is only an average. Averages can hide some fairly large differences in word learning. One study estimated that fifth-graders learned from 1,000 to nearly 5,000 new word meanings per year (White et al., 1990). This is a fairly large spread, with the most able learner learning five times as many new word meanings as those less able.

Why is there such a difference? One explanation for this is that good readers are better able to derive word meanings from context than poorer readers (Sternberg & Powell, 1983). But this does not seem to be the case. Two types of studies have been used to examine children's learning from context. The first set of studies had students derive a word's meaning from context. That is, students would be given a sentence such as "We needed to close the *kloptics* so the drapes would not fade," and be asked to determine what *kloptic* meant. In this task, more able students were better able to define the unknown word (Elshout-Mohr & van Daalen-Kapteijns, 1987; McKeown, 1985). However, the real task of word learning does not involve giving students sentences and having them derive these meanings. Instead, words are learned through chance encounters in the text. Unknown words are not signalled, nor are readers asked to come up with a definition immediately after reading. Instead, words are accumulated over time, through exposure and gradual learning (Schwanenflugel, Stahl, & McFalls, 1997). However, studies that examined *incidental* learning found that higher-ability students were not any better than lower-ability students at incidental word learning (Nagy, Anderson, & Herman, 1987; Nagy, Herman, & Anderson, 1995; Schefelbine, 1990; but also see Stanley & Ginther, 1991, who did find such differences). Instead, children of all abilities seemed to learn at about the same rate.

Training Children to Use Context. Additional evidence that there is little or no significant difference between high- and low-ability children learning words from context comes from studies to train children to become better at deriving word meanings from context. If there are ability differences in learning from context, then teaching children to be better at using context would also increase vocabulary. Kuhn and Stahl (in press) examined studies designed to teach students to be more efficient at learning from context. They failed to find evidence that children could be taught to improve their ability to derive words from context.

Kuhn and Stahl suggested that, if high and low ability students learned from context at about the same rate, then the difference in vocabulary growth might be due to differences in the amount that children read rather than differences in any ability to learn from context.

Matthew Effects. Because poor readers tend to read less than better readers, the gap between good and poor readers in absolute numbers of words read becomes progressively greater as the child advances through school. This is part of the *Matthew Effects* discussed by Stanovich (1986), who suggested that "the rich get richer and the poor get poorer" in vocabulary and other aspects of reading. That is, children who are good readers become better readers because they read more and also more challenging texts, but poor readers get relatively worse because they read less and also less challenging texts. Indeed, researchers have found large differences in the amount of free reading that good and poor readers do in and out of the school (Anderson, Wilson, & Fielding, 1988). In

Figure 4.
Hypothetical "Matthew Effects"

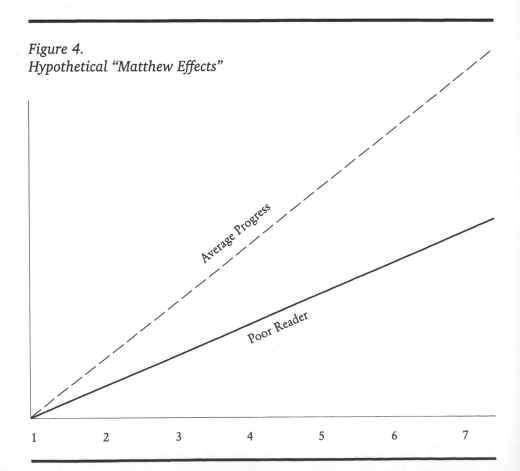

addition, the amount of reading that people do is directly related to their knowledge of word meanings, even after accounting for intelligence (Cunningham & Stanovich, 1991). This research as a whole suggests that the differences in children's word knowledge may be due largely to differences in the amount of text to which they are exposed.

One obvious way, then, to increase the number of words children know is to increase the amount of text to which they are exposed. Children with reading problems, however, are considered "reluctant" readers for good reasons. They read less than more able readers, simply because reading is more difficult for them. But, if they don't read more, then they are not going to become better readers. Many aspects of reading, including vocabulary knowledge, will suffer. Children who have difficulties in reading cannot make sense of the more challenging texts needed for growth in vocabulary. Without reading that more challenging text, they will not learn the vocabulary needed for the next most challenging text, and so on.

What Should We Do? It would be hard to argue against increasing the amount of reading that children do. Wide reading improves children's vocabulary knowledge. It also can improve children's overall intellectual growth (Cunningham & Stanovich, 1991).

Teaching word meanings can also improve children's comprehension (Stahl & Fairbanks, 1986). If one can teach 300 words per year, this will be a larger percentage of words for a child who might ordinarily learn 1000 words a year from context (White et al., 1990) than it would for a child who would ordinarily learn 3000 or 5000 words The answer must be a combination of both, including not only direct instruction of word meanings, but also discussions about words, including discussions of prefixes, suffixes, and roots, and wide reading, especially reading that challenges children's abilities (Chall, 1996).

Another way of providing that exposure to new vocabulary might be to read to children — even older children who are not traditionally read to. Several studies have found that children can learn words as efficiently from having stories read to them as they can from reading stories themselves. For example, Stahl, Richek, and Vandevier (1990) found that sixth-graders learned about as many word meanings from a single listening as they would learn from a single reading. This was especially true for children with lower vocabulary knowledge. Although word meanings can and should be learned through listening to stories, listening can only supplement and not supplant essential practice in reading.

Chapter 3

How Do People Learn Words from Context? And What Does It Mean to "Know" a Word?

We live in a sea of words. Most of these words are known to us, either as very familiar or at least as somewhat familiar. Ordinarily, when we encounter a word we don't know, we skip it, especially if the word is not needed to make sense of what we are reading (Stahl, 1991). But we remember something about the words that we skip. This something could be where we saw it, something about the context where it appeared, or some other aspect. This information is in memory, but the memory is not strong enough to be accessible to our conscious mind. As we encounter a word repeatedly, more and more information accumulates about that word, until we have a vague notion of what it "means." As we get more information, we are able to define that word.

How Do People Learn Words from Context?

Carroll (1964) argues that good vocabulary teaching should resemble the way that people learn words ordinarily, only more efficiently. The goal of vocabulary learning is to have students store the meanings of words in their long-term memory, and to store the kind of information about a word that is useful in understanding text. Since most words are learned from context, good vocabulary instruction should simulate learning from context. Learning from context, however, is a long-term process. Good vocabulary teaching should compress that process so that students can learn more words in a shorter period of time.

What happens when someone sees a word for the first time in a book? Consider the following paragraph from *The Atlantic Monthly*:

> America's permanent election campaign, together with other aspects of American electoral politics, has one crucial consequence, little noticed but vitally important for the functioning of American democracy. Quite

simply, the American electoral system places politicians in a highly vulnerable position. Individually and collectively they are more vulnerable, more of the time, to the *vicissitudes*[2] of electoral politics than are the politicians of any other democratic country. Because they are more vulnerable, they devote more of their time to electioneering, and their conduct in office is more continuously governed by electoral considerations. (King, 1997)

Although I had seen the word *vicissitudes* before, I did not know its meaning. From the context, one can get a general picture of what it means, something like "serendipitous happenings." My *Random House Dictionary* (1978) says "unexpected changing circumstances, as of fortune," so I was fairly accurate in my guess.

When a word is encountered for the first time, information about its orthography is connected to information from the context, so that after one exposure a person may have a general sense of the context in which it appeared ("It has something to do with ..."), or a memory of the specific context ("I remember seeing it in an automobile manual"), but not a generalizable sense of the meaning of the word. Dale and O'Rourke (1986, p. 3) talk about four "levels" of word knowledge:

1. I never saw it before.
2. I've heard of it, but I don't know what it means.
3. I recognize it in context — it has something to do with . . .
4. I know it.

In ordinary encounters with a word in context, some of the information that is remembered will be reinforced. The information that overlaps between encounters is what is important about the word. Other information will be forgotten. The forgotten information is more incidental. With repeated exposures, some connections become strengthened as that information is found in repeated contexts, and become the way the word is "defined."

Consider the word *vicissitudes* in the above context. The concept of *vicissitudes* will likely be linked to other concepts in the context, such as "politicians," "electoral politics," or possibly to the whole scenario presented. Because of the syntax, we know that *vicissitudes* does not directly mean "politics," but is a

---

[2] Emphasis added.

characteristic of politics. As the word is encountered repeatedly, it will be associated with other concepts, possibly "romance" or "getting a job." (Or as the
mother of one of my students told her repeatedly while growing up, "Beware of
the vicissitudes of life.") These become the strong components of the concept,
such as might be represented in a dictionary definition (McKeown, 1991). If
the links to other concepts are not repeated, they may recede in importance.
Given the core meaning of the word *vicissitudes*, the fact that the subject of the
essay is politics is incidental and likely would be forgotten with repeated exposures.

As a person encounters the word again and again, word meaning would
grow at a relatively constant rate, dependent on the features of the context.
Thus, people would show as much absolute gain in word knowledge from an
unknown word as they would from a word of which they have some partial
knowledge, all other things being equal (Schwanenflugel, Stahl, & McFalls, 1997).
We found that students made the same amount of growth in word knowledge
from a single reading, whether they began by knowing something about a word
or not. Thus, vocabulary knowledge seems to grow gradually, moving from the
first meaningful exposure to a word to a full and flexible knowledge.

One does not always need to know a word fully in order to understand it
in context or even to answer a test item correctly. Adults possess a surprising
amount of information about both partially known and reportedly unknown
words. Even when people would report never having seen a word, they could
choose a sentence in which the word was used correctly at a level above chance
or discriminate between a correct synonym and an incorrect one (Durso &
Shore, 1991). This suggests that people have some knowledge even of words
that they reported as unknown, and that this knowledge could be used to make
gross discriminations involving a word's meaning. Curtis (1987) found that
people who reported only a partial knowledge of a word's meaning ("I've seen
it before") could make a correct response to multiple-choice questions.

When young children learn words, they seem to learn what category the
word belongs to relatively quickly. Thus, children may learn that a word refers
to a "color" or an "animal" or a "toy" after a single exposure to the word,
gradually picking up more information with more exposures. This has been
called "fast mapping" (Heibeck & Markman, 1987; Rice, Buhr, & Nemeth,
1990). Fast mapping has been demonstrated with young children (Heibeck &
Markman, 1987) and with children with learning problems (Rice et al., 1990).
This suggests that definitions have a lot to teach us about words, or at least
words that are easily categorized. Words like *vicissitudes* do not fit well into

particular categories. As will be discussed in the next section, definitions may be confusing for these types of words. The importance of category information to young children suggests that definitions are an important part of what we know about words. However, definitional information alone is not sufficient to know a word.

Definitions

Traditionally, to know a word is to know its definition. However, this research suggests that people can understand enough about words to understand them in context without knowing a full definition. In fact, knowing a full definition may come only after a person knows a word fairly well.

Definitions, in fact, are conventions that we use to talk about words. There is a form for a definition, dating back to Aristotle, in which the definition first identifies which class (*genus*) the word belongs to, and then how that word differs from other members of its class (*differentia*). For example, The Random House Dictionary (1978) defines a *fissure* as "a narrow opening [the class] produced by cleavage [the differentiation]."

There is a great deal of research showing that children cannot use conventional definitions to learn words (Scott & Nagy, 1997). Perhaps the best illustration of the weaknesses of definitions comes from sentences children write after reading definitions. For example, for the following definition of *redress*:

> 1. set right; repair, remedy; *when King Arthur tried to redress wrongs in his kingdom.*

one student wrote:

> The *redress* for getting well [when] you're sick is to stay in bed (Miller & Gildea, 1987).

Another student wrote for *erode* (defined as "to eat out"):

> My family *erodes* often (Nist, personal communication).

Such subtle misunderstandings of word meanings from definitions, while humorous to the native speaker, illustrate the fact that a word's "meaning" is not captured fully in a description of its logical relations to other words, as in the Aristotelian dictionary definition. Instead, a word's meaning needs to be contextualized, so that the learner can see how it relates to other words in a conventional spoken or written context.

Some dictionaries depart from the traditional Aristotelian approach and more directly explain a word. The COBUILD English Language Dictionary (1995) explains words in a natural English by attempting to produce explanations of the word's use in ordinary English. For example, *delicate* is described as "Something that is delicate is fragile and needs to be handled carefully" (see also McKeown, 1993). *Lollop* is defined as "When an animal or a person lollops along, they run awkwardly and not very fast." *Lollop* is also described as a literary word, and an example sentence is given. The contrast between the COBUILD approach and ordinary dictionaries is instructive. Dictionaries based on the Aristotelian model do not teach words. Instead, they provide information about words in a conventional form. This conventional form is useful only after the word is encountered in context (Nist & Olejnik, 1995). The COBUILD approach creates a rich contextual usage containing enough definitional elements for the student to learn from the word. The effect is similar to having a person explain the word.

The difference between the conventional dictionary and the COBUILD approach is the difference between a student reading a definition and having someone explain it to him or her. All too often, teachers have had students look up words and expected the dictionary to provide the same information as a good explanation. Conventional dictionaries might be more useful *after* a person encounters a word in text, the way most adults use them (Nist & Olejnik, 1995). Thus, having students look up a set of words before reading a book might not be as useful as having a dictionary next to the student while they are reading. A good practice might be to assign dictionary work as a "during reading" activity. Students could be asked to use the dictionary to look up either words of their own choosing or words that the teacher chooses as they encounter them in their reading.

Memorizing definitions alone is also not likely to be effective. We found that just teaching definitions did not significantly affect children's reading comprehension (Stahl & Fairbanks, 1986). One study, for example, had students memorize short definitions, such as "Debris means trash," but it found they did no better on comprehending a passage containing the word *debris* than students who did not study the vocabulary in the passage.

The COBUILD[3] approach is what we do when we explain words, rather

---

[3] The COBUILD Dictionary is not without flaws. Because of its longer explanations, it appears to contain fewer words than conventional "college" dictionaries. It does not contain the word "paranomasia," my personal test for dictionary coverage. Nor does it provide etymological information.

than define them. Prior to reading, it may not be useful for children to read dictionary definitions. Rather, the teacher should provide explanations, similar to the COBUILD approach, of what a word really means. McKeown (1993) gives explanations of how to do this, but I think that nearly all teachers do this instinctively.

Contextual Knowledge

When a person "knows" a word, they know more than the word's definition; they also know how that word functions in different contexts. For example, the definition of the verb *smoke* might be something like "to inhale and puff the smoke of (a cigarette, etc.)" (Random House, 1978). However, the verb *smoke* describes distinctly different actions in the following sentences:

(a) He smoked a cigarette.
(b) The psychologist smoked his pipe.
(c) The hippie smoked a marijuana cigarette.
(d) The thirteen-year-old smoked his first cigarette.

These all fit under the general definition, but the actions vary from a typical smoking action in (a), to a puffing in (b), to a deeper and longer inhaling in (c), to an inhaling followed by coughing and choking in (d). Children cannot learn this information from a dictionary definition. Instead, they need to see the word in many different contexts, to see how the word meaning changes and shifts.

Thus, to understand the word in (d) we need to know that thirteen-year-olds are generally novices at smoking, and that smoking can make one cough, if one is not used to it. Similarly, to understand the words in the jargon-laden paragraph at the beginning of Chapter 1, a person needs to understand something about the domain of cognitive psychology and probably a bit about lexical semantics. Some words are embedded in a single knowledge domain, such as *dharma* or *jib*. To understand *dharma*, one must understand at least some basic concepts associated with Hinduism or Buddhism. To understand *jib*, one must know something about sailing. These words are so tied to their knowledge domains that they cannot be defined outside of them. (Some people, e.g., Johnston, 1985, have used vocabulary tests to measure domain knowledge.) Most words can be used in multiple domains but have distinct meanings within those domains. The word *obligation*, for example, has a series of related meanings, depending on whether the obligation is a moral one, or a payment due on a loan, and so on. Anderson and Nagy (1991) argue that words are polysemous, containing groups of related meanings, rather than a single fixed meaning. These meanings have a family resemblance to each other. Consider the word *give* in these different contexts (Anderson & Nagy, 1991, p. 700):

> *John gave Frank five dollars.*
> *John gave Mary a kiss.*
> *The doctor gave the child an injection.*
> *The orchestra gave a stunning performance.*

All of these involve some sort of transmitting, with a giver, a recipient, and something, tangible or intangible, that is given. But the act of giving is radically different in each case.

Nouns and Verbs

Teaching Verbs. Although we tend to talk about vocabulary as separate from grammar, they are, of course, connected. *Give*, for example, is a verb. In language, verbs function differently from nouns and modifiers (adjectives and adverbs). Each verb implies a frame that needs to be filled with nouns or noun phrases. For example, the verb *give* implies that there is a giver (subject), a recipient (indirect object) and a gift (direct object). Thus, a sentence like *John gave a present* would not be an acceptable sentence unless the context specified to whom John gave the present. Similarly, *John gave to Tim* would not be an acceptable sentence since we do not know what John gave to Tim. (Adding *"it"* would make it acceptable.) Other verbs require less specification. The verb *has* requires only a subject and a direct object (*John has a ball*). *Run* requires only a subject (*John ran* or *John ran to the post office.*). *Run*, in the sense of moving fast, cannot take a direct object. (There are other senses of *run* that can take a direct object, as in *John runs a threshing machine.*)

A verb is a frame for the sentence. Using a verb means filling in that frame with the appropriate grammatical categories. In learning words from context, people induce this information as one of the features of the word. With exposure to sentences containing verbs, people learn what is required, what is optional, and what is incompatible with that verb. In direct teaching, a teacher can point out how verbs direct the grammar of a sentence. Thus, in discussing a verb like *migrate*, the teacher might quickly mention that you need to know who migrated and where they migrated to. Where they migrated from is important, but may be implied by the context, or may not be necessary. For a more structured lesson, a teacher might display a sentence frame for each verb taught, such as:

_____ ameliorated _____.
WHO   WHAT

These can be done on cardboard with a window for the "Who" and the "What." Strips of nouns can be used for each window, and students can judge whether the resulting sentences make sense or are silly.

The use of verb frames can be complex, since some verbs take concrete nouns in some positions, while others can take either concrete or abstract nouns, etc. Many sentences can be correct grammatically, but make no sense. The classic example is Noam Chomsky's *Colorless green ideas sleep furiously*, which is "grammatical" in that it has a subject and a verb, but does not make sense because *sleep* cannot have an abstract noun as a subject.

Teaching Nouns. Nouns can be either concrete nouns (*brick, urn, amethyst*) or abstract (*truth, justice, the American way*). Concrete nouns can generally be pictured, e.g., *pliers*. Concrete nouns may also be described well with a word picture such as "A *cauldron* is a large pot, usually black and placed over a fire. Picture a group of witches, standing over a cauldron with a large stick, stirring a large amount of magic potion."

Abstract nouns, on the other hand, need many examples (and non-examples) before they are understood. Abstract nouns can be the most demanding part of teaching. Teaching a word like *liberty* may require a great deal of discussion of what might be examples of *liberty* (freedom to drive where you want to, freedom to choose your leaders, etc.) and non-examples of *liberty* (having to listen to your parents, living in a repressive society, etc.). Abstract nouns require a great deal of discussion, so that students can get the nuances of the term.

Multiple Meanings

Many words in English have multiple meanings. If we include shades of meanings or related meanings as multiple meanings, then nearly every word in English is in some way polysemous, since the meaning of a word changes subtly in different contexts (Anderson & Nagy, 1991). I will discuss three types of multiple meanings — metaphoric extensions, homonyms, and idioms. These three types of multiple meanings often confuse students, especially English-as-a-Second-Language students. Students, again especially ESL students, need to know that English is a flexible language. Often these students approach language as if it were math, so that one word is the precise equivalent of another word. This is not the case in any language. Words shift their meanings over time. For example, the word *line* originally came from an old French word meaning "linen" and referred to a thread from that fabric. From there, we got *line* meaning a distance between two points, a *line* of kings, a *line* of text, and at least 65 other meanings. These multiple meanings are usually metaphors based on the primary or a secondary meaning. For example, a "line of kings" compares the decedents of kings to a continuous line. (My unabridged dictionary gives a separate entry for *line* as in "to line a coat," although that meaning also derives from "linen.")

Metaphoric extensions are best taught through context. For *line*, any of the first entry meanings (from the straight line) would be apparent from context. A sensitive teacher might have to discuss how the word *line* changes its meaning in a sentence such as "He came from a long line of fishmongers," perhaps creating an image of great-grandfather, grandfather, father, and son all standing in a line, handing down a trade. The second meaning would have to be taught separately, as if it were a new word.

Idioms are expressions which have changed meaning over the years. Examples might be "to hem and haw," "in the same boat," "on the rocks," "sacred cow," "taken to the cleaners," and so on. Funk (1955) provides stories for a great many such idioms. These expressions present especial problems for ESL learners, who might have difficulty understanding, for example, why two people can be "in the same boat" when there is no boat mentioned. Again, idioms might be taught as if they were single words or might be taught using word stories, such as the following from Funk's book:

> Obviously, two or more people or things occupying one boat must share equal risk, and the phrase has thus acquired such figurative meaning; to share risks equally, to have identical obligations or involvements, to be in or live under similar conditions. Literary usage of the phrase goes back only about a hundred years, but it may have had its origin in an older expression, by three centuries, "to have an oar in another's boat," that is, to interfere or meddle with the affairs of another. (p. 98)

Word Stories. Telling word stories can make words memorable. Knowing that *bilious* comes from the medieval humor, *bile*, which caused anger, or knowing that a comedian's *patter* comes from the Latin *pater noster,* the beginning of the Lord's Prayer, makes the words more memorable. There are a number of books which are good sources of these stories. Among these are:

- Asimov, Isaac. *Words from the Myths* (1961, Boston: Houghton-Mifflin), *Words from Science and the History Behind Them* (1974, London: Harrup), or *Words on the Map* (1961, Boston: Houghton-Mifflin).
- Lederer, Richard. *The Miracle of Language* (1991, NY: Pocket Books), *Crazy English* (1989, NY: Pocket Books), or many other books, all of which are recommended.
- Funk, Charles Earl. *A Hog on Ice* (1985), *Thereby Hangs a Tale* (1950), or *Heavens to Betsy* (1955, all NY: Harper-Collins).
- Tjleja, Tad. *The Cat's Pajamas* (NY: Fawcett Columbine, 1987).
- Morris, William. *Morris Dictionary of Word and Phrase Origins* (1977, Harper and Row).
- Ciardi, John. *A Second Browser's Dictionary* (1983, NY: Harper and Row).
- Ayto, John. *Dictionary of Word Origins* (1990, NY: Ardace Publishing, Little Brown).
- Flexner, Stuart Berg. *Listening to America* (1982, NY: Simon & Schuster), or *I Hear America Talking* (1976, NY: Van Nostrand Reinhold).
- Hilliam, David. *Wordlore* (1984, Edinburgh, UK: Chambers).
- Lighter, Jonathan. *Random House Historical Dictionary of American Slang,* *Vol. I, A-G* (1994), *Vol. II, H-O* (1997).

I would recommend having some of these resources in one's library, to use for word stories in class. (They also are a lot of fun to read for one's own pleasure.)

In addition, some vocabulary development books include word stories or word origins. Among these are *Wordly Wise* (Cambridge, MA: Educator's Publishing Service), intended for grades 4–12, and *The World of Words,* by Margaret Richek (Boston: Houghton-Mifflin), intended for high school and college.

Palindromes and Paronomasia. Related to word stories is word play. Playing with words is a way of creating interest in words. Palindromes are words or phrases which are spelled the same backwards and forwards. Examples include phrases such as *Able was I ere I saw Elba* (never really said by Napoleon) and *Rats live on no evil star,* or words like *radar* or *Bob.*

Paronomasia is an obscure word meaning "puns." Puns are humorous unexpected switches in meaning. For example:

LIONEL: What's the difference between a teacher and an engineer?

TYRONNE: A teacher trains minds; an engineer minds trains.

In this pun, multiple meanings of both *train* and *mind* are combined. Although many believe that "All punsters should keep their gags in their mouths," puns can interest children in words. Consider the following as a word lesson:

> A man goes into a bar. He's sitting on the stool, enjoying his drink, when he hears "You look great!" He looks around — there's nobody near him. He hears the voice again. "No really, you look terrific."
>
> The man looks around again. Nobody. He hears, "Is that a new shirt or something? Because you are absolutely glowing." He then realizes that the voice is coming from a dish of nuts on the bar.
>
> "Hey," the man calls to the bartender. "What's with these nuts?"
>
> "Oh," says the bartender, "they're complimentary."

This groaner reinforces the meaning of "complimentary" as well as any direct teaching. Since students usually repeat jokes, even bad ones, the repetition might make the word more memorable.

The following variations on foreign phrases imported to English can interest students in the original phrases or in finding new phrases to change. These were reportedly winners in a *New York Magazine* contest in which contestants were to take a well-known expression in a foreign language, change a single letter, and provide a definition for the new expression.

> HARLEZ-VOUS FRANÇAIS? (Can you drive a French motorcycle?)
>
> IDIOS AMIGOS (We're wild and crazy guys!)
>
> COGITO EGGO SUM (I think; therefore I am a waffle.)
>
> or COGITO, ERGO SPUD (I think, therefore I yam.)
>
> RIGOR MORRIS (The cat is dead.)
>
> RESPONDEZ S'IL VOUS PLAID (Honk if you're Scottish.)
>
> QUE SERA SERF (Life is feudal.)
>
> LE ROI EST MORT. JIVE LE ROI. (The king is dead. No kidding.)
>
> PRO BOZO PUBLICO (Support your local clown.)
>
> VENI, VIDI, VICE (I came, I saw, I partied.)

And one more:

> A man was shipwrecked on an island. On one side of the island was a tall tree in which nested a family of myna birds. The tree was surrounded by a group of large, stately lions. The lions didn't bother the man,

unless he approached them. Then the stately lions would growl and bare their teeth.

One day a group of talking porpoises swam up to the shore of the island. The man begged the porpoises to get him off the island. The porpoises agreed, but demanded that the man bring them each a myna bird from the nest in the tall tree.

After much thought, the man fashioned a pole and vaulted over the stately lions into the tree, where he grabbed the nest of mynas, and pole vaulted back over the stately lions.

He gave the myna birds to the porpoises, and they ate them. When the man asked why they ate the myna birds, the leader of the porpoises replied "We're immortal. We must eat the myna birds to stay immortal." The porpoises then carried the man back to his home.

The next day, the man was awakened by the police, who had come to arrest him. Angrily, the man demanded to know with what crime he was being charged.

The officer replied, "Transporting mynas across stately lions for immortal porpoises."

Puns probably do not add much to a student's knowledge of specific words. Instead, I think that puns (and other word play) serve to interest students in the world of words. James Joyce observed that "puns were the highest form of humor" because they involve thinking about how words sound and what words mean in different ways. A true "groaner" such as the myna-lion-porpoise joke above requires a person to think about words in ways outside of their ordinary use in language. Flexibility in dealing with language should affect a person's more serious use of words. Interest in language cannot help but expand a person's world.

Full and Flexible Knowledge

A full and flexible knowledge of a word involves an understanding of the core meaning of a word and how it changes in different contexts. To know a word, we not only need to have *definitional knowledge*, or knowledge of the logical relationship into which a word enters, such as the category or class to which the word belongs (e.g., synonyms, antonyms, etc.). This is information similar to that included in a dictionary definition. In addition, we also need to understand how the word's meaning adapts to different contexts. I have called this *contextual knowledge*, since it comes from exposure to a word in context. This involves exposure to the word in multiple contexts from different perspectives. Children exposed to words in multiple contexts, even without instruction, can be presumed to learn more about those words than students who see a word in a single context (Nitsch, 1978; Stahl, 1991).

A full and flexible understanding of a word is more than a definition, but also more than the information one gets out of context. It is important to remember that for some words, in some circumstances, a person does not need to know everything about a word to comprehend it in a context. For *vicissitudes*, a little knowledge may be enough not to interfere with comprehension, and that is all one needs. For words that embody key concepts, in biology or social sciences for example, one may need to teach words more extensively. To understand genetics, concepts like *DNA* need to be taught well.

The next two sections will review first, general principles for teaching words, and next, specific techniques for teaching concepts in content areas.

Chapter 4

General Principles for Teaching Words

The Usefulness of Context

A number of authors have suggested lists of context clues (e.g., Ames, 1966). However, explicit context clues are rarely available in natural text. Instead, contexts vary tremendously in their "helpfulness" or how much information they provide the reader. Beck, McKeown, and McCaslin (1983) suggest four levels of helpfulness. Contexts can be *directive*, where they provide explicit and detailed information about the word; *generally directive*, where they provide general information about the word; *nondirective*; or *misdirective*. An example of a directive context in which the meaning is explicitly signalled is:

> When the cat pounced on the dog, he leapt up yelping and knocked
> down a shelf of books. As the noise and confusion mounted, Mother
> hollered upstairs, "What's all that *commotion?*"

In the following example of a generally directive context, the context is compatible with the meaning, but yields many possible meanings for *gregarious*, including "popular," "happy," and so on.

> Sam and Joe came to the party together. By 9:30, it seemed like a drag
> for Sam, but Joe seemed to be enjoying himself. "I wish I could be as
> *gregarious* as Joe," thought Sam.

A nondirective context, such as the following, gives less information about a word's meaning. The italicized word could mean anything from "dainty" to, well, "lumbering."

> Dan wondered who had arrived. He couldn't make out any voices. But
> then he heard the *lumbering* footsteps of Aunt Grace.

A misdirective context is one which leads to misunderstandings. In the following context, one would probably expect a meaning such as "admiringly":

> Sandra had won the dance contest. "Every step she takes is so perfect,"
> Ginny said *grudgingly.*

Contrary to common belief, most contexts are nondirective at best or misdirective at worst. Schatz and Baldwin (1986) found that most contexts provide little help in figuring out a word's meaning. Consider the following two contexts from their study:

> No one would deny the _____ advantages, both cultural and civic, of such arts districts. Atlanta's Midtown Business Association of real estate interests and businessmen points out that four million visitors flock to the district each year for arts-related events. "The arts are up on a level with religion and education," says association president Hiram Wilkinson.

> Just about the time when the Allied troops were liberating Europe from the Nazi _____, American forces were routing the Japanese from their captured Pacific possessions. By the end of February 1945, the Philippines were liberated by General MacArthur.

These are natural contexts, the first from *Newsweek*, the second from a history text, typical of everyday reading. Few people could come up with *pragmatic* for the first blank and *yoke* for the second, although both do make good sense. These, and most of the contexts reviewed by Schatz and Baldwin, would be considered as either nondirective or misdirective. In textbooks, authors often will add a parenthetical phrase to define a word, or enrich the context so that a potentially difficult word can be understood by a student audience. This is not so in ordinary writing. When authors use words, they choose those words because they are the most apt. Uncommon words like *pragmatic* or *yoke* are chosen because they carry the nuance of meaning the author intends. Authors writing for a general audience (not just for students) will not provide clues about uncommon words. Therefore, in real-world reading, most contexts are not particularly helpful for getting the exact meaning of an unknown word.

We reviewed the research on techniques of teaching people to learn from context, using lists of context clues, cues, specific strategies, or general guidance in how to learn from context (Kuhn & Stahl, 1998). No approach was found to be successful in improving incidental learning from context, without being told specifically to do so, nor were specific teaching programs markedly better than mere exhortations to use context. Because learning from context is a natural process, teaching children to derive word meanings from context may be superfluous, or teaching them something they already know how to do. Since children already have some prowess in learning words from context and must have implicit strategies to do so, it is possible that these learning from context strategies may merely allow children to verbalize better what it is that they are already doing. If so, these children may do better on a measure that requires verbalization of this ability, but may not show any overall improvement in the skill. In other words, they may be better able to talk about what they are doing, but may not be able to do it better.

Kuhn and Stahl (1998) recommend that children read widely and in material that will provide challenging words. As noted earlier, children learn an average of 3000 new words per year. This number dwarfs the 300 to 600 that can be reasonably taught directly. Therefore, increasing the amount of reading that children do maybe the most reliable way of improving children's vocabulary, more so than specific teaching techniques. Indeed, Anderson, Fielding, and Wilson (1988) found that increasing the amount of reading that children did outside of school, using a "Book Flood" approach, did significantly improve children's vocabulary. In a Book Flood, the school sends books home, provides incentives for reading, and so on in order to dramatically increase the amount of reading that children do.

In addition to providing opportunities for wide reading, one needs to sensitize children to the importance of learning words from context. The Word Wizard activity, used by Beck et al. (1992), is one option. As teachers encounter and discuss unusual words (a more common activity in literature-based classrooms in which books with no vocabulary control are used), they add the words to a Word Wizard chart. If a child sees the word again and notes the context, his or her name goes up on the chart. There can be periodic awards for being a "Word Wizard." I have seen this implemented in a second-grade classroom. Children enjoyed looking for words such as *palindrome, beret,* or *container* and developed an appreciation for unusual words. They also chose the words for the Word Wizard chart from words heard in stories read by the teacher.

Another way of sensitizing readers to word meanings is using a *knowledge rating checklist* (Blachowicz, 1986; Dale & O'Rourke, 1986). In a knowledge rating checklist, children check their knowledge of words, asking themselves whether they know a word well enough to define it, have seen or heard it and have a general sense of its meaning, or have never seen or heard it. Such checklists can be used in whole-class settings. One such checklist is the one in Figure 5 on the next page.

All recommendations of how to teach word meanings need to be tempered

Figure 5.
A knowledge rating checklist.

WEATHER
How much do I know about these words?

	Can define	Have Seen/heard	Don't Know
Airmass	✓		
Air Pressure	✓		
Meteorology			✓
Humidity		✓	
Barometer		✓	
Front	✓		
Anemometer			✓

From Blachowicz (1986).

by the overwhelming importance of wide reading. This does not mean that we should not teach words directly. As noted earlier, children learn 3000 words per year on average. White and his colleagues (1990) found children learned a range of between 1000 and 5000 new words a year. At the lower end of that range, a gain of 300 words is a 30% gain, a significant improvement. Even at the average levels, an improvement of 10% is probably educationally significant, especially if improvements of 10% are sustained over several years. Therefore, direct vocabulary teaching should be a part of a child's reading program.

Three Principles of Vocabulary Development

Because vocabulary instruction is an ongoing process, a teacher needs to be able to vary the delivery of that instruction. This involves using different approaches during the school year. Our model of effective vocabulary instruction suggests vocabulary instruction that (a) includes both definitional information and contextual information about each word's meaning, (b) involves children more actively in word learning, and (c) provides multiple exposures to meaningful information about the word. These will be discussed below.

Include Both Definitional and Contextual Information. As noted earlier, our knowledge of a word's meaning involves more than knowing a definition. People also need to know how a word functions in different contexts. Stahl and Fairbanks (1986) found that approaches providing only definitional information did not significantly affect children's reading comprehension. In contrast, methods that provided both definitional and contextual information did significantly improve comprehension.

Some things that a teacher might do to provide definitional information include:

(1) *Teaching synonyms.*

(2) *Teaching antonyms.* Not all words have antonyms, but thinking about antonyms requires a child to, first of all, identify the crucial aspects of a word. For example, a word like *pandemonium*[4] implies lawlessness, or clutter, but its antonym, *order*, focuses the meaning on the "chaos" part of the word's meaning,

(3) *Rewriting definitions.* Having students state a definition in their own words is more powerful than having them remember the exact wording of the definition. Definitions can be confusing to children (Scott & Nagy, 1997). Having children restate definitions may be the only way a teacher can find out whether they can understand them.

(4) *Providing examples* is another way for a teacher to ascertain whether students understand definitions. These examples may be drawn from personal experiences ("My room is pandemonium.") or from school content ("After the Civil War, there was pandemonium all over the South.").

(5) *Providing non-examples* requires the student to think about the critical attributes of a word, similar to the task of providing antonyms.

(6) *Discussing the difference between the new word and related words.* For example, a discussion of the word *debris*, defined as "trash" or "waste," might include a discussion of the differences between *debris* and *trash* ("trash" could include anything; "debris" results after some sort of accident or disaster), *garbage* (generally refers to organic material, such as food leftovers), or *waste* (implies something left over, rather than something resulting from a disaster). Such a rich discussion focuses the meaning of the word. (This can be similar to semantic mapping, discussed later.)

---

[4] In its modern sense, not in the Miltonian sense of the home of the demons.

Similarly, a teacher could provide contextual information by:

(1) *Having students create sentences containing the target word.* Sentences should show the meaning clearly, and cannot be vague. Sometimes it is useful to ask students to use more than one word in each sentence. Using more than one word in a sentence forces students to look for relations among words.

(2) *Discussing the meaning of the same word in different sentences.* It is important that a teacher use multiple sentences, so that a student is not locked into a particular context. If possible, the contexts should be as varied as possible. For the word *pandemonium,* sentences might include topics such as chaos in the classroom, chaos in terms of clutter and mess, chaos in relations among people, etc.

(3) *Creating a scenario.* This involves more than a sentence, but making up a complete story. An alternative for younger children might be drawing a picture story for a new word.

(4) *Silly questions.* Beck, Perfetti, and McKeown (1982) used silly questions in their vocabulary lessons. This involves pairing the words being taught and creating a question out of each pair. For the words *actuary, hermit, philanthropist,* and *villain,* a set of questions might include "Can an actuary be a hermit? Can an actuary be a philanthropist? Can a philanthropist be a hermit? Can a philanthropist be a villain?"

Involve Children in Actively Processing New Word Meanings. A second principle of effective vocabulary instruction relates to how active students are at constructing links between new information and previously known information. Children remember more information when they are performing cognitive operations on that information (Craik & Tulving, 1975). Such operations might include relating it to known information, transforming it in their own words, generating examples, non-examples, antonyms, synonyms, etc. Stahl and Fairbanks developed the following scale of processing that is useful for evaluating vocabulary instructional programs:

• *Association processing* involves the rote memorization of an association between a word and its meaning or between a word and a single context.
• *Comprehension processing* in which the child demonstrates comprehension of an association by reading it in a sentence or by doing something with the definitional information, such as finding an antonym, classifying words, etc.

- *Generative processing* in which the child takes the information learned and creates a new product or a novel response to the word, including creating a sentence which fully expresses the word's meaning, restating a definition in one's own words, etc. This product could be written or oral.

Stahl and Fairbanks (1986) found that generative processing did lead to better retention of word meanings, but the effects on comprehension were not as clear. Generative processing did lead to improvements in comprehension only when children were given multiple exposures to different information about word meanings.

Beck and her colleagues (Beck et al., 1982; McKeown, Beck, Omanson, & Perfetti, 1983; McKeown, Beck, Omanson, & Pople, 1985) examined the effects of generative processing with multiple exposures. Lessons in the Beck et al. (1982) study, for example, were conducted in a five-day cycle. On the first day, words were defined. Then, students discussed how each word is used in context. This discussion could take a number of different forms, including discussion of examples and non-examples, pantomimes, or having students say "Yea" if the word is used correctly in a sentence or "Boo" if it is not. On the second day, after a review of the definitions, students might have worked on log sheets, completing sentences for each word. On the third day, students completed another worksheet with the vocabulary words and then work on a "Ready, Set, Go" activity. This is a timed activity in which pairs of students attempt to match the words with their definitions in the shortest amount of time. This activity was repeated on the fourth day. After completion of the second "Ready, Set, Go," students were asked silly questions, pairing two of the concepts together, such as "Can a *virtuoso* also be a *rival?*" On the fifth day, students took a post-test.

These are only examples of activities, which varied somewhat with different units. Students also completed a "Word Wizard" activity each day. They were given credit toward becoming a "Word Wizard" by finding examples of each word used outside of class.

This program, or variations of it, was found to significantly improve students' comprehension of texts containing words that were taught. In addition, McKeown, Beck, Omanson, and Pople (1985) found that twelve encounters with a word reliably improved comprehension, but four encounters did not. They also found that their approach, which involved active processing of each word's meaning, had significantly greater effects than the definition-only approach on measures of comprehension but not on measures involving the recall of definitions. Thus, their research suggests that vocabulary instruction can improve comprehension, but only if the instruction is rich and extensive, and includes a great many encounters with to-be-learned words.

Use Discussion to Actively Teach Word Meanings. Discussion adds an important dimension to vocabulary instruction. First of all, children benefit from the contributions of other children. It is our experience that children who enter a vocabulary lesson without any knowledge of a target word seem to learn a great deal from their peers, who may have partial or even fairly good knowledge of the word. We have found that in open discussions children are often able to construct a good idea of a word's meaning from the partial knowledge of the entire class. (When the class as a whole does not know much about a word, however, the teacher may have to interject some information about the word, such as a quick definition.)

Discussion can clarify misunderstandings of words by making them public. For words that a child partially knows, or knows in one particular context, the give-and-take of discussion can clarify meanings. When misunderstandings are public, the teacher can shape them into the conventional meaning.

In addition, discussion seems to involve children in other ways. While waiting to be called upon, students practice or prepare a response to themselves. Even though only one child is called upon, many children anticipate having to come up with an answer. Because many children are practicing a response covertly, discussion seems to lead to increased vocabulary learning (Stahl & Clark, 1987). Because of the importance of each child expecting to be called upon, teachers should allow all children in the class some think time before calling on one individual (Rowe, 1974). Also, a teacher should be sensitive to his or her patterns of calling on children, avoiding just calling on the "fast" kids. A child who does not think that s/he will be called upon will not practice a response. Without the practiced response, discussion is not as valuable a learning experience (see Alvermann, Dillon, & O'Brien, 1987).

Limitations. Although vocabulary instruction does seem to significantly improve comprehension, at least when the words being taught are in the text, there are some limitations. Teaching vocabulary can, under certain circumstances, distract a reader from the main ideas in the text. One study found that teaching words that were associated with low-level information encouraged students to focus on that information. Because students were focusing on unimportant details, they were not as good at recalling important information as students who did not get vocabulary instruction (Wixson, 1986). Thus, it is important that a teacher choose words which are important to the ideas in a text, rather than words that are interesting but not related to the main ideas of a story or passage.

A Sample Lesson

To put these concepts together, consider how one might teach the following words, taken from the story "The Talking Eggs" by Robert San Souci: *backwoods, contrary, dawdled, groping, rubies, silver*. For *backwoods*, one might read the sentence from the story — "Then the old woman took her by the hand and led her deep into the backwoods." I would ask students to predict what *backwoods* meant. This word is a compound and should be fairly clear from the word parts, combined with some context. Students could be asked to describe the backwoods briefly.

Similarly, to teach *contrary* I would begin, again, with the sentence from the book — "You do as I say and don't be so contrary" — and ask students to predict its meaning. I would then discuss a definition, such as "disagreeable, raising objections" and how it fits into that sentence. Next, students might provide some sentences which use *contrary*. I might also discuss the other related meaning for *contrary*, that of "from another point of view" as in the expression *to the contrary*.

For *rubies* and *silver*, we might discuss what precious things are, and possibly provide pictures of *rubies* and of *silver*. Together, the class and I could make a list of precious things, including *rubies* and *silver*, as well as *gold, diamonds*, etc.

Groping and *dawdled* are verbs. I might begin again with the sentences in the story, and also do a pantomime, rather than provide merely a verbal definition. Then, students would add their own sentences. I would suggest some nonexamples for *dawdled*, since it seems to be a word that has some clear antonyms, such as *hustled, ran, went quickly*, and so on.

The words above are highly dissimilar, grouped together only because they happen to come out of the same story. This is often the case in literature-based classrooms. The techniques used to teach the words are somewhat similar. For four of the six words, I started with the text sentence. I chose that sentence to make a link to the text. Then I asked for additional sentences to extend the meaning of the word beyond the text. Finally, I also included a definition, either a verbal or a gestural one, for all of the words. Otherwise, I tried to adopt my instruction to the words, using the general principles discussed above.

This is relatively minimal instruction, designed to support the reading of the text. More elaborate instruction might include additional sentence contexts for each word, a "yea or nay" activity ("Would you dawdle in the backwoods?"), having students write a scenario containing these words, and so on. Minimal instruction would keep the focus on the story. More elaborate instruction would shift the focus from the story to the vocabulary, and might be useful in a classroom with a great many ESL learners or in other situations where a greater emphasis on vocabulary is appropriate.

Chapter 5

Procedures For Teaching Word Meanings As Concepts

The principles discussed in the previous chapter — including both definitional and contextual information, involving children actively in learning new word meanings, and using classroom discussion — can be used to adapt existing vocabulary instruction so that it is more effective. For example, if a teacher is using materials which have students find new words in a dictionary or glossary and write down their definitions, that teacher might add an exercise involving generating sentences and a class discussion of the sentences students made up. If a teacher is examining the meaning of a word found in context, s/he might have students generate different scenarios which use the word or rephrase the definition.

The principles discussed in the previous chapter are useful for adapting and extending individual vocabulary learning exercises. However, often a teacher needs to teach complex concepts, such as *DNA, independence, quadratic equation,* and so on. Complex concepts require multidimensional teaching techniques. This chapter reviews a number of such techniques below.

Semantic Mapping. In Semantic Mapping, one targeted word is tied through the discussion and the mapping to other related words (Heimlich & Pittelman, 1986). Semantic Mapping instruction begins with the teacher presenting a central concept and having students brainstorm or freely associate words that are related to that concept. These are all written on the blackboard. During this brainstorming, the teacher adds words that need to be learned. For example, for one unit on "Weather," the teacher targeted the words *meteorology, global, precipitation, barometer,* and *hurricane* from a text the children were about to read (Stahl & Vancil, 1986). These words were defined and discussed during the brainstorming session. When the children were finished, the teacher and the class together developed a map showing the relationships between the words, highlighting the target words (see Figure 6 on the next page). One section was left blank so that the class could fill in another category after reading.

Figure 6.
Semantic Mapping

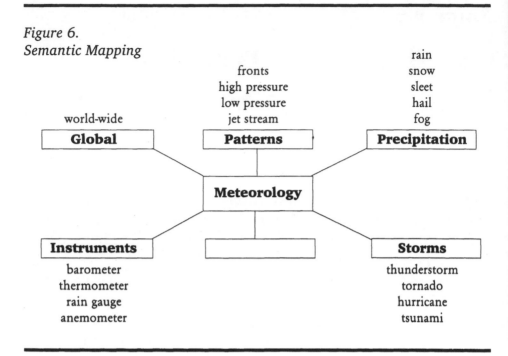

Semantic Mapping is highly flexible and adaptable to a number of different contexts. I have seen it used to teach such diverse things as polygons, the Dewey Decimal system, and music terms (see Heimlich & Pittelman, 1986).

Semantic Mapping has been found to effectively improve both children's recall of taught words and their understandings of passages containing taught words in a number of different circumstances (Johnson, Toms-Bronowski, & Pittelman, 1982; Johnson, Pittelman, Toms-Bronowski, & Levin, 1984; Margosein, Pascarella, & Pflaum, 1982). Pittelman, Levin, and Johnson (1985) found that it worked equally well with whole classes and small groups.

The discussion seems to be a crucial element in the effectiveness of Semantic Mapping (Stahl & Clark, 1987; Stahl & Vancil, 1986). An individualized mapping procedure, in which students studied maps on their own, did not work as well as a group procedure. As noted earlier, discussion in Semantic Mapping instruction seems to engage children by making them rehearse possible answers. One study found that children who knew they were not going to be called upon in class did not recall as many word meanings as children who thought they might be called on (Stahl & Clark, 1987). This was true, even though all children could listen to the same discussion.

Discussion may be especially important for the children who begin with lower vocabularies. For the high vocabulary children, most of these related words are known, and thus reinforce the target words. For the low vocabulary children, more of the related words may be unknown, and thus may be learned as well. As noted earlier, Marmolejo (1991) found that approaches such as Semantic Mapping are especially effective for poor readers.

Semantic Feature Analysis. Similar to Semantic Mapping, Semantic Feature Analysis draws upon students' prior knowledge, using discussion to include information about word meanings into a graphic display. Semantic Feature Analysis uses a grid (such as the one in Figure 7, below) rather than a map, but otherwise the two seem to be similar. Down the left side, the teacher should write the names of members of the class of concepts. Across the top, write feature terms. For a unit on transportation, one might place terms such as *car, truck, bicycle, ship, taxi, velocipede, unicycle, dirigible, space shuttle* down the side and *flies, motor, "footpower," wheels, rocket, public, private, land, sea, air* across the top. Students should be encouraged to add terms either across the top or down the side during discussion. I like to have classes discuss whether each item is an example of each concept, marking "+" for positive examples, "-" for negative examples, and "?" for items which could be examples under certain circumstances. As with Semantic Mapping, discussion seems to be key in this activity, since, in my experience, there are many ambiguities. Discussion of the ambiguities seems to clarify the concepts.

Figure 7.
Semantic feature analysis for Transportation

	two wheels	four wheels	one wheel	foot power	motor power	on land	in the water	in the air
bicycle	+	-	-	+	-	+	-	-
car	-	+	-	-	+	+	-	-
unicycle	-	-	+	+	-	+	-	-
airplane								
boat								
hovercraft								
supersonic transport								
velocipede								

Semantic Feature Analysis and Semantic Mapping also were found to have similar effects by Johnson, Toms-Bronowski, and Pittelman (1982). Anders, Bos, and Filip (1984) found that Semantic Feature Analysis significantly improved poor high school readers' learning of word meanings and comprehension of a social studies passage, effects which persisted when tested nine months later (Anders, Bos, & Filip, 1984).

Semantic Grouping. Semantic Mapping and Semantic Feature Analysis, as well as the program developed by Beck and her colleagues and discussed earlier (e.g., Beck et al., 1982) all chose to teach words in semantic groups. In Beck et al.'s program, one unit taught "People" words such as *virtuoso, novice, hermit, rival, philanthropist, tyrant, miser,* and *accomplice,* while another group stressed "Things you can do with your arms," and so on. Some authors (e.g., Nagy, 1988) suggest that all words should be taught so that there is a common relation among the words in a lesson.

The rationale for grouping words in semantic categories comes loosely from studies of adults' knowledge of concepts, which suggests that words are stored in long-term semantic memory in *semantic networks* (e.g., Collins & Loftus, 1975). In these models of memory, concepts are stored in nodes, which are connected to other nodes by various links, including logical relations. So a concept like *shark* might be connected to *fish,* as well as to related concepts such as *man-eating, hammerhead,* the movie *Jaws,* and so on (see Figure 8 on the next page). One can answer questions such as "Do sharks have gills?" through one's knowledge that sharks are fish, even if one does not know for a fact that sharks do have gills. This view of knowledge as an organized, structured domain has developed into *schema theory* (see, e.g., McNeil, 1987). Schema theory suggests that a person's knowledge store influences the way that one learns information, as well as a person's ability to make inferences. Thus, a text does not have to say that a shark lives in the ocean, since that can be inferred by the knowledge that a shark is a fish.

If words are stored in categories, then it makes sense to teach them that way. And teaching words in semantic categories has been recommended by a number of different authorities (e.g., Graves, 1986; Johnson & Pearson, 1986; McNeil, 1987; Nagy, 1988). However, the studies which tested this directly have found mixed results. Durso and Coggins (1986) found that some aspects of grouping led to better word learning, but only on some measures. The general vocabulary treatment used in the Durso and Coggins study, memorizing definitions, was one that had not been found to be effective in improving perfor-

Figure 8.
Semantic grouping for "shark"

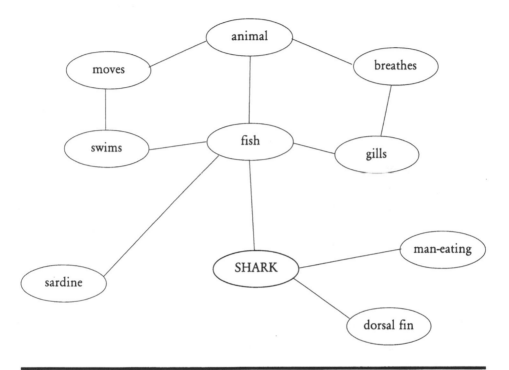

mance on comprehension tasks (Stahl & Fairbanks, 1986). Stahl, Buridge, Machuga, and Stecyk (1991), using a richer form of vocabulary instruction, found that children learned words equally well whether they were learned in groups or not. They suggest that children are going to draw associations among words when given rich vocabulary instruction and may not need to learn words in groups. This finding suggests that teachers need not choose words to form semantic groups, but can instead choose words more freely from texts, as long as they provide rich and varied vocabulary instruction for those words.

Given rich and elaborate instruction, Semantic Grouping *per se* may not be necessary, at least in all circumstances. Semantic Grouping is, however, an important component of a number of approaches to teaching word meanings, including Semantic Mapping and Semantic Feature Analysis. In addition, Marmolejo (1991) found that approaches that teach word meanings as part of a semantic field were especially effective for children with low initial vocabularies. Such students may need help tying new word meanings to already existing word knowledge.

Possible Sentences. Another approach to teaching word meanings is the development of Possible Sentences. In the Possible Sentences activity, the teacher first chooses about six to eight words which might cause difficulty for the students. In a content area text, these words are usually key concepts in the text, but they also may be more general words that relate to those key concepts. Then, an additional four to six words are chosen that are more likely to be known by the students. These are used to help generate sentences. In our study, for example, we chose *front, barometer, humidity, air mass, air pressure,* and *meteorology* as the target words for a unit on weather, with *high, rain, clouds,* and *predict* as the contrast words (Stahl & Kapinus, 1991). We chose the target words based on our intuition about which words might be difficult for fifth-graders, and because these words were central to the concepts taught in the passages. The contrast words were words we thought would be known to the students and would lend themselves to logical sentences which would relate to the major concepts in the chapter.

These ten to twelve words are then put on the board. Teachers can provide a short definition of each word if desired or necessary. Most of the time at least one student in the class has knowledge of the word that can be shared. Students are directed to think of sentences containing at least two of these words and which might be in the chapter (or passage) they are about to read. Student contributions are then put on the board. Both accurate and inaccurate guesses are included, and are not discussed at this time. When the students are finished contributing sentences (and all words are included in at least one sentence), the teacher has them read the passage or chapter.

Following the reading, the teacher then returns to the sentences on the board, and the class as a whole discusses whether each sentence could or could not be true based on their readings. If a sentence could be true, it is left alone. If a sentence could not be true, then the class discusses how it could be modified to make it true.

Stahl and Kapinus (1991) found that Possible Sentences significantly improved both children's recall of word meanings and their comprehension of text containing those words. This was true when compared to a control and also when compared to Semantic Mapping.

By requiring that children use two words in each sentence, the teacher requires them to understand the relations between the words. Such information tends to be definitional in nature. Through discussion and evaluation of the sentences, children are forced to actively process semantic information about each word.

Concept Development Approaches. Yet another approach to teaching word meanings comes from the studies of children's concept development. Based on the model of Frayer (Frayer, Fredrick, & Klausmeier, 1969), Wixson (1986) taught children groups of words by (a) identifying the critical attributes of the word, (b) giving the category to which it belongs, (c) discussing examples of the word, (d) discussing non-examples of the word. For example, for the word *prehistoric*, students discussed why dinosaurs were prehistoric animals and lions were not, what prehistoric people might have worn, recognized a definition for prehistoric [before written history], discussed whether stone hammers and steel hammers were prehistoric tools, and wrote a definition of *prehistoric* in their own words. She found that such a procedure improved comprehension of passages containing the taught words.

Schwartz and Raphael (1985) transformed this general procedure into Word Maps or Concept of Definition Maps, which were used to teach children elements commonly found in definitions (see Figure 9). Their intention was to use these word maps to help children learn new word meanings from context, in addition to being used to directly teach new words. This approach does appear successful in teaching new words, but its effectiveness in helping children become better at learning word meanings from context is questionable. However, as discussed earlier, it is not clear whether any instructional approach has unequivocally improved children's learning of word meanings from context (Kuhn & Stahl, 1998).

Figure 9.
Concept-of-definition map for "computer"

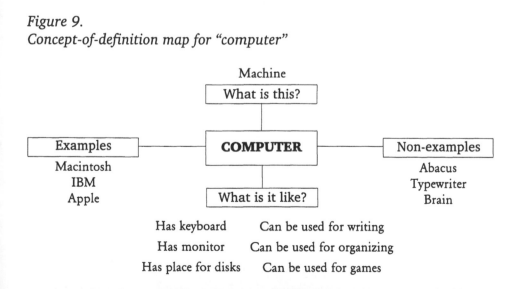

Comparing and Contrasting. Often it is important to compare and contrast two different concepts. For example, when teaching the American Revolution, it is important to contrast *protest* and *rebellion.* The colonists thought they were protesting the English taxes by acts such as the Boston Tea Party. In contrast, King George III thought the colonists were rebelling. The difference in perceptions led to increasing tensions and, eventually, revolution. A simple Venn diagram, such as the one in Figure 10 below, can be a good teaching tool for such contrasts. This diagram can be used to contrast such things as *bacteria* and *viruses, monocots* and *dicots, symphony* and *concerto, republic* and *democracy,* etc. One can also make diagrams or charts that distinguish characteristics (*respects authority, challenges authority*) from examples (*Vietnam War protests, marches*).

Teaching Word Parts

Another type of productive vocabulary instruction involves the teaching of within-word parts, or prefixes, suffixes, and roots. While words like *geologist, interdependent,* and *substandard* can often be figured out from context, decomposing such words into known parts like *geo-, logist, inter-, depend,* etc., not only makes the words themselves more memorable, but, in combination with sentence context, may be a useful strategy in determining the meaning of unknown words (Dale & O'Rourke, 1986). This strategy may be especially important for content-area reading, where many of the words contain identifiable

Figure 10.
Venn diagram for "protest" and "rebellion"

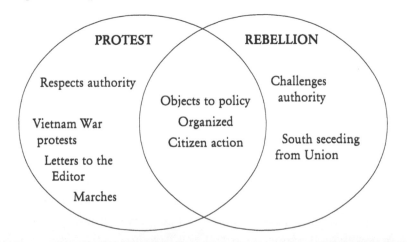

word parts whose meanings are the same in many different words.

How do children acquire the meanings of word parts that might aid in determining the meanings of unknown words? One possibility is that they infer them during reading. However, while such a process may be part and parcel of normal reading, a number of studies (e.g., Sternberg & Powell, 1983; O'Rourke, 1979) provide evidence that even many high school students are unaware that decomposing words into their parts can help with deriving their meanings, and often students do not know the meanings of common word parts. Thus, less able readers might benefit from instruction in this area.

What Parts to Teach? One must first decide which parts are worth teaching. One can find exhaustive lists containing hundreds of prefixes, suffixes, and Greek and Latin roots (e.g., Dale & O'Rourke, 1986; Fry, Fountoukidis, & Polk, 1985). Although such lists may be useful, it hardly seems possible or even fruitful to teach each element on each list. It would seem most useful to both directly teach the most commonly used or important elements and teach a general strategy for decomposing words. Such a strategy would teach a student to combine word-part information with information from the sentence context.

Prefixes. White, Sowell, and Yanagihara (1989) found that only twenty prefixes accounted for 97% of prefixed words that appear in printed school English, excluding those that were followed by non-English roots (such as the *ad-* in *adjacent*). They concluded that teaching at least the top nine (if not all twenty) to middle school students would pay dividends in increased vocabulary learning. They found that third-graders who were given training on these nine prefixes and a strategy for decomposing words into roots and suffixes outperformed a control group on several measures of word meaning.

Suffixes. White et al. also estimated the frequency of suffixes in printed school English (shown in Figure 11 on the next page). Inflectional endings such as noun endings (*-s, -es*), verb endings (*-ed, -ing, -en*), and adjective endings (*-er, -est*) were the most common. In general, these are used in even young children's oral language, and should not be a problem for middle school and older children.

Derivational suffixes appear in fewer than a quarter of all the words that contain suffixes, but they might be useful to teach. Comprehension of relatively infrequent words such as *exponential* and *unwieldy* can be aided by knowledge of the *-ial* and *-y* suffixes. Many children, especially poorer readers, have difficulty isolating the root word. Knowledge of which letter patterns are suffixes may also serve to help poor readers identify the root. Often such children are overwhelmed by the length of words. Giving them a word part reduces the

Figure 11.
The Most Frequent Affixes in Printed School English

Rank	Prefix	% of All Prefixed Words	Suffix	% of All Suffixed Words
1.	*un-*	26	*-s, -es*	31
2.	*re-*	14	*-ed*	20
3.	*in-, im-, il-, ir- (not)*	11	*-ing*	14
4.	*dis-*	7	*-ly*	7
5.	*en-, em-*	4	*-er, -or (agent)*	4
6.	*non-*	4	*-ion, -tion, -ation, -ition*	4
7.	*in-, im- (in)*	3	*-able, -ible*	2
8.	*over-*	3	*-al, -ial*	1
9.	*mis-*	3	*-y*	1
10.	*sub-*	3	*-ness*	1
11.	*pre-*	3	*-ity, -ty*	1
12.	*inter-*	3	*-ment*	1
13.	*fore-*	3	*-ic*	1
14.	*de-*	2	*-ous, -eous, -ious*	1
15.	*trans-*	2	*-en*	1
16.	*super-*	1	*-er (comparative)*	1
17.	*semi-*	1	*-ive, -ative, -tive*	1
18.	*anti-*	1	*-ful*	1
19.	*mid-*	1	*-less*	1
20.	*under- (too little)*	1	*-est*	1
	All Others	3	*All Others*	1

From White, Sowell, and Yanagihara (1989).

size of the word and allows them to focus in on relevant information within the word (Adams, 1990). This is a natural extension to decoding instruction which teaches children to look at chunks of words. Compare/contrast decoding approaches, such as that of Cunningham (1995), have children look at a word such as *enlistment*, and verbalize a strategy of comparing chunks of the words to known, shorter words. For example, *enlistment* might be decoded as "If *ten* is 'ten,' then *en* is 'en.' If *fist* is 'fist,' then *list* is 'list.' And if *ten* is 'ten,' then *ment* is 'ment.' By putting it together we can get en-list-ment, *enlistment*." Teaching suffixes seems to be the next step beyond such a decoding strategy.

Other suffixes, such as *-ful* or *-less*, are meaningful components of words, contributing to words' meanings in much the same way that prefixes do. Even suffixes without such stable meanings, such as *-tion* or *-ly*, might also help identify words, if only to cue the reader in on the grammatical function of words in sentences. For example, *-tion* indicates that a word is a noun; *-ly* at the end of a word indicates that a word is an adverb.

Roots. When children encounter unknown words like *interdependent, readable,* and *substandard,* they can analyze the words for structural elements, including prefixes, suffixes, and familiar English roots, and combine these within-word cues with conceptual information in the context. But what about content words like *biology, extraterrestrial, geologist,* and *projectile?* In addition to their prefixes or suffixes, they also contain Greek or Latin *roots*.

Reading educators are divided as to whether to teach these roots or not. Nagy and Anderson (1984) argue that the modern meanings of words (especially the most common derived words) often do not reflect the meanings of their historical roots, and that readers might be misled by a literal translation of root to meaning. For example, knowing *-mort* refers to "death" may help with *mortal* or *immortal,* but probably does not help a person guess the meaning of *mortgage* or *mortify.* The Oxford English Dictionary (available on-line through our library and others) gives the following quote to explain the relationship between *mort* and *mortgage:*

> *1628 Coke On Litt. 205* It seemeth that the cause why it is called mortgage is, for that it is doubtful whether the Feoffor will pay at the day limited such summe or not, & if he doth not pay, then the Land which is put in pledge vpon condition for the payment of the money, is taken from him for euer, and so dead to him vpon condition, &c. And if he doth pay the money, then the pledge is dead as to the Tenant, &c;]

Mortify has an even more interesting history, moving from "put to death" in the 14th century, to "bruise," to "destroy the vitality of or to neutralize the effect of," to "to bring into subjection the appetites of the body by self-denial," and finally "to cause a person to feel humiliated." This word, in itself, is a case study of how language changes over time.

Likewise, knowing *saline* will not help with *salary*, even though they are both derived from the same root. (Salt was once so valuable that it was used to pay workers.)

On the other hand, teaching roots may make the words more memorable by adding a story to the word's definition. Research has found that having children elaborate basic information makes it more memorable (Pressley, 1988). For example, *sanguinary* and *sanguine* both derive from the Latin word meaning "blood," but *sanguinary* means "bloodthirsty" and *sanguine* (by way of the Middle Ages' belief that body fluids affected one's disposition) means "cheerful." I heard this example in high school and have remembered both the meanings and the example since.

Figure 12 on the next page presents a list of commonly occurring Greek and Latin roots. For individual content areas, it might be worthwhile to make up lists specific to each area. Thus, for biology, such a list might include *bio*, *chromo*, *eco*, *soma*, etc.

How to Teach Word Parts

Introductory lessons in word part lessons should stress the idea that words can be composed of elements, such as prefixes, suffixes, and roots. These should be defined for the students, but the emphasis should not be on learning the specific terms as much as on learning about how parts function together to affect word meaning. For example, a lesson on *un-* might not only provide examples of words beginning with *un-*, but also ask students to generate *un-* words of their own, including silly words. The use of imaginative extensions may not only solidify the meaning of *un-*, but also may solidify the concept of *prefix* in general. Non-examples of prefixes, such as *under* and *uncle*, also help reinforce the basic concept of prefixing.

One distinction that should be made is between English roots (such as *depend* in *interdependent*) and Greek or Latin roots (such as *cred* in *incredible*). Looking for common English words within longer words and parsing out prefixes and suffixes might be a useful strategy for many words. Since poor readers tend to be overwhelmed by long words, they may need to be taught how to do

Figure 12.
Common Greek and Latin roots in English

Root	Meaning	Origin	Examples
aud	hear	Latin	*audiophile, auditorium, audition*
astro	star	Greek	*astrology, astronaut, asteroid*
bio	life	Greek	*biography, biology*
dict	speak, tell	Latin	*dictate, predict, dictator*
geo	earth	Greek	*geology, geography*
meter	measure	Greek	*thermometer, barometer*
min	little, small	Latin	*minimum, minimal*
mit, mis	send	Latin	*mission, transmit, remit, missile*
ped	foot	Latin	*pedestrian, pedal, pedestal*
phon	sound	Greek	*phonograph, microphone, phoneme*
port	carry	Latin	*transport, portable, import*
scrib, script	write	Latin	*scribble, manuscript, inscription*
spect	see	Latin	*inspect, spectator, respect*
struct	build, form	Latin	*construction, destruct, instruct*

this. For example, a teacher might teach students to attack *interdependent* by teaching them to cover the prefix *inter-* to see if the rest of the word is recognizable. If not, then covering the suffix *-ent,* and leaving *depend* might make it easier. Practice in adding and removing prefixes and suffixes might also be useful. For example, a teacher might take the base *dependent* and add prefixes such as *in-* or *non-* to make new words.

After the basic concepts of prefix, suffix, and root are known, teaching specific word parts should be easier. This can be done within the context of other vocabulary instruction, as part of the discussion of a particular word's meaning, or using direct instruction. Such instruction would include a definition for the target word part, models of words using that word part, and reading sentences containing the target parts. For prefixes, one should attempt to extend the instruction to include as many real and silly words as possible. For *un-*, we not only have *unclean, unimaginable* or *uninformed,* but the *Uncola, unhamburger, unsleep,* and so on.

This strategy could be done for suffixes as well. While prefixes should be defined, since their definition tends to be consistent over a variety of words, definitions of suffixes may confuse children. Some sources define *-ance/-ence* and *-ment* as "condition of, quality of, or state of." Adding this to the definition of a root might make understanding *amendment* or *precedence* a complicated task indeed. Instead, many examples of words containing suffixes might be given, along with the words they were derived from. Ample experience with both the suffixed words and the original words would probably be more useful than memorizing an abstract definition.

For roots, similar teaching procedures could be employed. It also might be useful to use a web such as that in Figure 13, below. Such webs would introduce children to many new words while teaching a few target words. Nagy and Anderson (1984) suggest that such a strategy of discussing derivatives when introducing a new word, with or without a web, is useful and motivational. Including words that are relatively infrequent (such as *geocentric* or *geode*) may make target words (such as *geology*) more memorable.

Clearly there are benefits to be gained from teaching children to decompose words into their parts as a strategy for determining the meanings of unknown words. When combined with the use of context clues, decomposition seems to be especially fruitful, particularly in the content areas since so many of the words encountered in content area texts contain recognizable parts.

Figure 13.
Word part web for the root "photo"

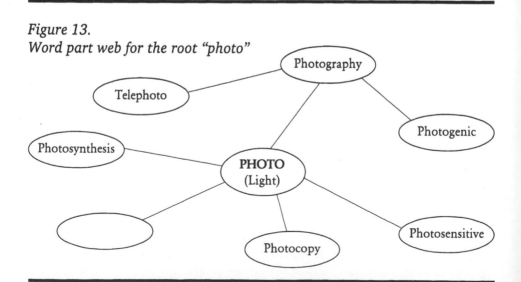

Chapter 6

Teaching Word Meanings

The techniques presented in this book were chosen because research supports their use. Other techniques might also be as effective. Since vocabulary development is an ongoing process, vocabulary instruction is a long term process. To avoid boredom, varied techniques need to be used. Therefore, an effective program of vocabulary instruction might include not only these approaches, but as many others as possible.

Which approaches you use to teach a word would depend on a number of factors. First, it would depend on the word itself. If a word's meaning seems fairly self-evident, like *backwoods*, you might provide relatively minimal instruction. For words that are more complex, such as *independence*, you might provide more complex instruction, such as a Concept of Definition Map. If the words in the lesson belong to the same semantic field, you might use instruction which takes advantage of those commonalities. Semantic Mapping, Semantic Feature Analysis, and Comparing and Contrasting techniques might be useful for words which fit together. You might adopt the same techniques if the words form the core concepts of a chapter in a science or social studies text.

Second, you might want to use techniques that are productive — that is, they teach more words than just the targeted words. There are circumstances where it is necessary to teach words one by one. In preteaching words to help children read a particular story, it may be best to focus on a small set of words from that story. To go beyond that set might distract children from reading the story. However, it is generally beneficial to teach words so that students learn more than just single words. If students need to learn the word *geology*, it can be taught with other words that share the same root (*geocentric, geodesic*) or the same suffix (*psychology, biology, sociology, sociobiology*). One can also teach geology as part of a semantic field, using a semantic map. Showing the links between *geology* and *rocks, expeditions*, etc., not only teaches the concept of geology, but also can reinforce other words associated with that concept. Both of these techniques, teaching a word that shares similar word parts with other words and teaching words in a semantic field, not only teach the targeted word, but also related words. In addition to learning the words that the teacher wants to teach, the student learns that each word is part of a universe of words, connected to other words by etymology and by connections between meanings.

Last, teaching words should be enjoyable. Pantomiming a verb such as *dawdled* should entertain. The active discussion of words in a Semantic Mapping lesson can be engaging. Debating whether a *space shuttle* has a rocket or a motor should keep students involved. Distinguishing between *garbage* and *trash* should lead to an "aha" of recognition. Telling word stories and learning the roots in words is enjoyable for adults as well as students. Words such as *retromingent, minatory,* and *plangent* are fun to use and a challenge to locate in an unabridged dictionary. Learning to use a word such as *beret* instead of *hat,* or *pusillanimous* instead of *cowardly,* should make a child think that he has learned a secret code — a better, more mature way to talk and write. After all, teaching word meanings should be a way for students to define their world, to move from *light* or *dark* to a more fine-grained description of the colors that surround us.

References

Adams, M.J. (1990). *Beginning to read: Thinking and learning about print.* Cambridge, MA: M.I.T. Press.

Alvermann, D.E., Dillon, D.R., & O'Brien, D.G. (1987). *Using discussion to promote reading comprehension.* Newark, DE: International Reading Association.

Ames, W.S. (1966-67). The development of a classification scheme of contextual aids. *Reading Research Quarterly, 2,* 57-62.

Anders, P.L., Bos, C.S., & Filip, D. (1984). The effect of semantic feature analysis on the reading comprehension of learning disabled students. In J. Niles & L.A. Harris (Eds.), *Changing perspectives in research in reading/language processing and instruction* (Vol. 33,). Rochester, NY: National Reading Conference.

Anderson, R.C., & Freebody, P. (1981). Vocabulary knowledge. In J.T. Guthrie (Ed.), *Comprehension and teaching: Research reviews* (pp. 77-117). Newark, DE: International Reading Association.

Anderson, R.C., & Nagy, W.E. (1991). Word meanings. In R. Barr, M.L. Kamil, P. Mosenthal, & P.D. Pearson (Eds.), *Handbook of Reading Research, Vol. II.* White Plains, NY: Longman.

Anderson, R.C., Wilson, P.T., & Fielding, L.G. (1988). Growth in reading and how children spend their time outside of school. *Reading Research Quarterly, 23,* 285-303.

Beck, I.L., McKeown, M.G., &, & McCaslin, E.S. (1983). All contexts are not created equal. *Elementary School Journal, 83,* 177-181.

Beck, I.L., Perfetti, C.A., & McKeown, M.G. (1982). Effects of long-term vocabulary instruction on lexical access and reading comprehension. *Journal of Educational Psychology, 74,* 506-521.

Berlin, B., & Kay, P. (1969). *Basic color terms: their universality and evolution.* Berkeley, CA: University of California Press.

Betts, E.A. (1946). *Foundations of reading instruction.* New York: American Books.

Bismonte, A.R. (1994). Effectiveness of the possible sentences vocabulary strategy with middle school students in Guam. *Reading Improvement, 31*(4), 194-199.

Blachowicz, C.L.Z. (1986). Making connections: Alternatives to the vocabulary notebook. *Journal of Reading, 29,* 643-649.

Carroll, J.B. (1964). Words, meanings, and concept. *Harvard Educational Review, 34*(2), 178-202.

Chall, J.S. (1995). *Readability revisited: The new Dale-Chall readability formula.* Cambridge, MA: Brookline Books.

Chall, J.S. (1996). American reading achievement: Should we worry? *Research in the Teaching of English, 30,* 303-310.

Collins COBUILD English Language Dictionary (1987). London: Collins

Collins, A.M., & Loftus, E.E. (1975). A spreading activation theory of semantic processing. *Psychological Review, 82,* 407-428.

Craik, F.I.M., & Tulving, E. (1975). Depth of processing and the retention of words in episodic memory. *Journal of Experimental Psychology: General, 104,* 268-294.

Cunningham, A.E., & Stanovich, K.E. (1991). Tracking the unique effects of print exposure in children: Associations with vocabulary, general knowledge, and spelling. *Journal of Educational Psychology, 83,* 264-274.

Cunningham, P.M. (1995). *Phonics they use.* New York: Harper Collins.

Curtis, M.E. (1987). Vocabulary testing and vocabulary instruction. In M.G. McKeown & M.E. Curtis (Eds.), *The nature of vocabulary acquisition.* Hillsdale, NJ: Erlbaum.

D'Anna, C.A., Zechmeister, E.B., & Hall, J.W. (1991). Toward a meaningful definition of vocabulary size. *Journal of Reading Behavior, 23,* 109-122.

Dale, E., & O'Rourke, J. (1986). *Vocabulary building.* Columbus, OH: Zaner-Bloser.

Durso, F.T., & Coggins, K.A. (1986). *Semantic fields and vocabulary: Acquisition, comprehension, and production.* Paper presented at the annual meeting of the Psychonomic Society.

Durso, F.T., & Shore, W.J. (1991). Partial knowledge of word meanings. *Journal of Experimental Psychology: General, 120,* 190-202.

Fodor, J.A., Garrett, M.F., Walker, E.C., & Parkes, C.H. (1980). Against definitions. *Cognition, 8,* 283-367.

Frayer, D.A., Frederick, W.C., & Klausmeier, H.J. (1969). *A schema for testing the level of concept mastery (Working Paper No. 16).* Madison, WI: University of Wisconsin, Wisconsin Research and Development Center for Cognitive Learning.

Fry, E.B., Fountoukidis, D.L., & Polk, J.K. (1985). *The new reading teacher's book of lists.* Englewood Cliffs, NJ: Prentice-Hall.

Gouldman, R., Nation, P., & Read, J. (1990). How large can a receptive vocabulary be? *Applied Linguistics, 11,* 341-363.

Graves, M.F. (1986). Vocabulary learning and instruction. In E.Z. Rothkopf (Ed.), *Review of Research in Education* (Vol. 13, pp. 49-91). Washington, DC: American Educational Research Association.

Harris, A.J., & Sipay, E. (1990). *How to increase reading ability.* (10th ed.). White Plains, NY: Longman.

Hayes, D.A., & Tierney, R.J. (1982). Developing readers' knowledge through analogy. *Reading Research Quarterly, 17,* 256-280.

Heibeck, T.H., & Markman, E.M. (1987). Word learning in children: An examinatino of fast mapping. *Child Development, 58,* 1021-1034.

Heimlich, J.E., & Pittelman, S.D. (1986). *Semantic mapping: Classroom applications.* Newark, DE: International Reading Association.

Herman, P.A., Anderson, R.C., Pearson, P.D., & Nagy, W.E. (1987). Incidental acquisition of word meanings from expositions with varied text features. *Reading Research Quarterly, 23,* 263-284.

Hirsh, D., & Nation, P. (1992). What vocabulary size is needed to read unsimplified texts for pleasure? *Reading in a Foreign Language, 8,* 689-696.

Johnson, D.D., & Pearson, P.D. (1986). *Teaching reading vocabulary.* New York: Holt, Rinehart, Winston.

Johnson, D.D., Pittelman, S.D., Toms-Bronowski, S., & Levin, K.M. (1984). An investigation of the effects of prior knowledge and vocabulary acquisition on passage comprehension (Program Report 84-5). Madison, WI: Wisconsin Center for Educational Research, University of Wisconsin.

Johnson, D.D., Toms-Bronowski, S., & Pittelman, S.D. (1982). *An investigation of the effectiveness of semantic mapping and semantic feature analysis with intermediate grade children (Program Report 83-3).* Madison, WI: Wisconsin Center for Educational Research, University of Wisconsin.

Johnston, P. (1984). Prior knowledge and reading comprehension test bias. *Reading Research Quarterly, 19,* 219-239.

Konopak, B.C. (1988). Effects of inconsiderate vs. considerate text on secondary students' vocabulary learning. *Journal of Reading Behavior, 20,* 5-24.

Kuhn, M.R., & Stahl, S.A. (in press). Teaching children to learn word meanings from context: A synthesis and some questions. *Journal of Literacy Research.*

Lorge, I., & Chall, J.S. (1963). Estimating the size of vocabularies of children and adults: An analysis of methodological issues. *Journal of Experimental Education, 32*(2), 147-157.

Margosein, C.M., Pascarella, E., & Pflaum, S. (1982, April). The effects of instruction using semantic mapping on vocabulary and comprehension. Paper presented at annual meeting of the American Educational Research Association, Chicago, IL.

Marmolejo, A. (1991, April,). *The effects of vocabulary instruction with poor readers. Paper presented at annual meeting, American Educational Research Association.*, Chicago, IL.

McKeown, M.G., Beck, I.L., Omanson, R.C. & Perfetti, C.A. (1983). The effects of long-term vocabary instruction on reading comprehension: A replication. , *15*(1), 3-18.

McKeown, M.G. (1991). Learning word meanings from dictionaries. In P. Schwanenfluegel (Ed.), *The psychology of word meanings*. Hillsdale, NJ: Lawrence Erlbaum Associates.

McKeown, M.G. (1993). Creating effective definitions for young word learners. *Reading Research Quarterly, 27*, 16-31.

McKeown, M.G., Beck, I.L., Omanson, R.C., & Pople, M.T. (1985). Some effects of the nature and frequency of vocabulary instruction on the knowledge and use of words. *20*, 522-535.

McNeil, J.D. (1987). *Reading comprehension: New directions for classroom practice.* (2nd ed.). Glenview, IL: Scott-Foresman.

Miller, G., & Gildea, P. (1987). How children learn words. *Scientific American, 257*(3), 94-99.

Nagy, W.E. (1988). *Teaching vocabulary to improve reading comprehension.* Newark, DE: International Reading Association.

Nagy, W.E., & Anderson, R.C. (1984). How many words are there in printed school English? *Reading Research Quarterly, 19*, 304-330.

Nagy, W.E., Anderson, R.C., & Herman, P.A. (1987). Learning word meanings from context during normal reading. *American Educational Research Journal, 24*, 237-270.

Nagy, W.E., & Herman, P.A. (1987). Breadth and depth of vocabulary knowledge: Implications for acquisition and instruction. In

M.G. McKeown & M.E. Curtis (Eds.), *The nature of vocabulary acquisition* (pp. 19-36). Hillsdale, NJ: Lawrence Erlbaum Associates.

Nagy, W.E., Herman, P.A., & Anderson, R.C. (1985). Learning words from context. *Reading Research Quarterly, 20*, 233-253.

Nist, S.L., & Olejnik, S. (1995). The role of context and dictionary definitions on varying levels of word knowledge. *Reading Research Quarterly, 30*, 172-193.

Nitsch, K.E. (1978). *Structuring decontextualized forms of knowledge.* Unpublished Ph.D., Vanderbilt.

O'Rourke, J. (1979, April,). *Prefixes, roots, and suffixes: Their testing and usage. Paper presented at annual meeting, International Reading Assocation.* Paper presented at the International Reading Assocation, Atlanta, GA.

Oxford English Dictionary (1989). Oxford, England: Oxford University Press.

Pittelman, S.D., Levin, K.M., & Johnson, D.D. (1985). *An investigation of two instructional settings in the use of semantic mapping with poor readers.* Madison, WI: Wisconsin Center for Educational Research, University of Wisconsin.

Pressley, M. (1988). *Elaborative interrogation.* Paper presented at annual meeting, American Educational Research Association, New Orleans, LA.

Random House Dictionary. (1978). New York: Random House.

Rice, M.L., Buhr, J.C., & Nemeth, M. (1990). Fast mapping word-learning abilities of language-delayed preschoolers. *Journal of Speech and Hearing Disorders, 55*, 33-42.

Rowe, M.B. (1974). Wait time and rewards as instructional variables, their influence on language, logic, and fate control — Part One: Wait time. *Journal of Research in Science Teaching, 11*, 81-94.

Schatz, E.K., & Baldwin, R.S. (1986). Context clues are unreliable predictors of word meaning. *Reading Research Quarterly, 21*, 439-453.

Schefelbine, J. (1990). Student factors related to variability in learning word meanings from context. *Journal of Reading Behavior,* 22, 71-97.

Schwanenflugel, P.J., Stahl, S.A., & McFalls, E.L. (1997). *Partial word knowledge and vocabulary growth during reading comprehension* (Research Report No. 76). University of Georgia, National Reading Research Center.

Schwartz, R.M., & Raphael, T. (1985). Concept of definition: a key to improving students' vocabulary. *The Reading Teacher, 39,* 198-203.

Scott, J.A., & Nagy, W.E. (1997). Understanding the definitions of unfamiliar verbs. *Reading Research Quarterly, 32,* 184-200.

Snow, C.E. (1990). The development of definitional skill. *Journal of Child Language, 17,* 697-710.

Stahl, S.A. (1991). Beyond the instrumentalist hypothesis: Some relationships between word meanings and comprehension. In P. Schwanenfluegel (Ed.), *The psychology of word meanings* (pp. 157-178). Hillsdale, NJ: Lawrence Erlbaum Associates.

Stahl, S.A., Burdge, J.L., Machuga, M.B., & Stecyk, S. (1992). The effects of semantic grouping on learning word meanings. *Reading Psychology.*

Stahl, S.A., & Clark, C.H. (1987). The effects of participatory expectations in classroom discussion on the learning of science vocabulary. *American Educational Research Journal, 24,* 541-556.

Stahl, S.A., & Fairbanks, M.M. (1986). The effects of vocabulary instruction: A model-based meta-analysis. *Review of Educational Research, 56*(1), 72-110.

Stahl, S.A., & Kapinus, B.A. (1991). Possible sentences: Predicting word meanings to teach content area vocabulary. *The Reading Teacher, 45.*

Stahl, S.A., Richek, M.G., & Vandevier, R. (1991). Learning word meanings through listening: A sixth grade replication. In J.

Zutell & S. McCormick (Eds.), *Learning factors/teacher factors: Issues in literacy research, Fortieth yearbook of the National Reading Conference* (pp. 185-192). Chicago: National Reading Conference.

Stahl, S.A., & Vancil, S.J. (1986). Discussion is what makes semantic maps work. *The Reading Teacher, 40,* 62-67.

Stanley, P.D., & Ginther, D.W. (1991). The effects of purpose and frequency on vocabulary learning from written context of high and low ability reading comprehenders. *Reading Research and Instruction, 30*(4), 31-41.

Stanovich, K.E. (1986). Matthew effects in reading: Some consequences of individual differences in the acquisition of literacy. *Reading Research Quarterly, 21,* 360-407.

Sternberg, R.J. (1987). Most words are learned from context. In M.G. McKeown & M.E. Curtis (Eds.), *The acquisition of word meanings* (pp. 89-106). Hillsdale, NJ: Lawrence Erlbaum Associates.

Sternberg, R.J., & Powell, J.S. (1983). Comprehending verbal comprehension. *American Psychologist, 38,* 878-893.

Terman, L.M. (1916). *The measurement of intelligence.* Boston: Houghton-Mifflin.

Thorndike, E.L. (1917). Reading as reasoning: A study of mistakes in paragraph meaning. *Journal of Educational Psychology, 8,* 323-332.

White, T.G., Graves, M.F., & Slater, W.H. (1990). Growth of reading vocabulary in diverse elementary schools: Decoding and word meaning. *Journal of Educational Psychology, 82.*

White, T.G., Sowell, J., & Yanagihara, A. (1989). Teaching elementary students to use word-part clues. *The Reading Teacher, 42,* 302-309.

Wixson, K.K. (1986). Vocabulary Instruction and Children's Comprehension of Basal Stories. *Reading Research Quarterly, 21*(3), 317-29.

Zakaluk, B.L., & Samuels, S.J. (1988). *Readability: Its past, present, & future.* Newark, DE: International Reading Association.

Index

About the Author

Steven A. Stahl is a Professor of Reading Education at the University of Georgia. He was formerly a principal investigator at the National Reading Research Center and at the Center for the Study of Reading at the University of Illinois. After teaching reading in elementary schools in New York and Maine, he received his doctorate in reading from the Harvard Graduate School of Education. His research interests are centered around issues in reading instruction at the primary grades and the relationship between vocabulary knowledge and reading comprehension.